Diamonds for Lori and Me

Books by Ralph Schoenstein

Diamonds for Lori and Me
Every Day Is Sunday
Alma Matters
The I-Hate-Preppies Handbook
East Versus West
Citizen Paul
Yes, My Darling Daughters
Wasted on the Young
I Hear America Mating
Little Spiro
My Year in the White House Doghouse
With T-Shirts and Beer Mugs for All
Time Lurches On
The Block

Diamonds for Lori and Me

A Father, a Daughter, and Baseball

Ralph Schoenstein

BEECH TREE BOOKS
WILLIAM MORROW
New York

Library of Congress Cataloging-in-Publication Data

Schoenstein, Ralph, 1933–
Diamonds for Lori and me: a father, a daughter, and baseball.
I. Title.
PS3569.C525D54 1988   813'.54   88-6258
ISBN 0-688-07897-4

Printed in the United States of America

BOOK DESIGN BY ELLEN LEVINE

The word "book" is said to derive from *boka*, or beech.
The beech tree has been the patron tree of writers since ancient times and
represents the flowering of literature and knowledge.

For Loren

Who has always belonged
with Lori and me

Contents

1. Some Loveliness That Lasts   *13*

2. The One-Sewer Man and the .700 Girl
   -Lori and I Discover The Game-   *19*

3. Giants and Pygmies
   -We Start to Love the National League-   *37*

4. Fear and Trembling at Second Base
   -The Family Position Is Claimed-   *59*

5. The Son of Vince Lombardi
   -Tossing Daughters into the Fray-   *83*

6. We Don't Care If We Never Get Back
   -The Grass Is Always Greener at Shea-   *107*

7. If They Don't Win, It's a Shame
   -But Still Better Than a Stanley Cup-   *149*

8. And Suddenly It's Spring
   -Beyond the Medals, The Game-   *167*

"The ball I threw while playing in the park
Has not yet reached the ground."

—DYLAN THOMAS

Diamonds for Lori and Me

1
Some Loveliness That Lasts

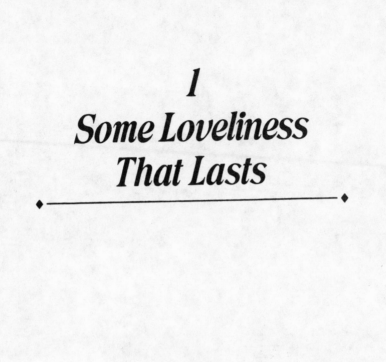

This too shall pass.

A happy thought for a kidney stone, but not for the best times of my life. It is three o'clock in the morning and once again I am facing the void. It is the Hour of the Wolf, which I meet with the heart of the chicken as I reel in despair at the fleeting nature of things. The good moments keep disappearing like dreams, while the terrors keep coming in fresh assaults.

An ancient Greek said, "All is flux," and how I wish he had been writing copy for a new soap instead of telling me that the only permanent condition is change. If nothing lasts, then nothing matters; and if nothing matters, then why did I produce three daughters and fifteen books and a play for the sixth grade about yellow fever, in which Walter Reed says, "The *fever* may be yellow, but *I'm* red, white, and blue!"

Buckle down, Winsocki. Hang on, Sloopy.

While hanging on, I remember some words I have written, my agnostic's prayer:

Dear God, who may not exist,
Guide me through the chaos
For sanity's sake.

If God does not exist, then life is a jumble of accidents, some lovely, some dreadful. Desperately, I try once more to embrace the lovely ones, to find something to hold on to, some loveliness that lasts.

Deciding to leave this bed of philosophical nails, I get up and walk down the hall. On the walls are photos of my wife and daughters and me taken during the last twenty-five years, and again I feel panic at drifting farther and farther from these sweet frozen frames. Turning away from them with a sigh, I go quickly out to the porch for some air. It is a summer night to savor: the tall trees, silhouetted against a full moon, are bending in a pine-scented breeze. Is there some message out here? While seeking it, I suddenly remember that whoever made these great backlit trees made the AIDS virus too, and soon may be hurling at us the kind of meteor that killed the dinosaurs. A man who remembers the Dionne quintuplets and Dolf Camilli, *I* will be a dinosaur hit by the next one.

Now badly needing the sight of beauty that is more than botanical, I go back into the house and walk to the bedroom of my youngest daughter, Lori, who has just turned eleven. As I enter the room, I stub my toe on a blue batting helmet and I smile at her cluttered little shrine to the Mets. On her closet is a big red K that she waved at Shea Stadium while begging Dwight Gooden to strike out every Cub; and near the helmet, strewn on a Mets T-shirt, are packs of bubble gum that she uses to make sticky salutes to Roger McDowell, whom she calls her Bubble Baby because his gum breaks as often as his curve. Lori, of course, is *my* Bubble Baby, for I keep fearing that her precious childhood is about to burst.

I want to wake her up and tell her that we beat the Cardinals tonight and Bubble Baby got the save; but she will find out tomorrow at breakfast when she reads *The New York Times* sports section instead of her homework, the only child majoring in box scores. She will find out that her darling HoJo hit a 3-and-1 pitch into the upper deck a few minutes after she fell asleep; and she will not be surprised: she knows that 3-and-1 is a hitter's pitch and HoJo got one of his beloved fastballs. *The Times* will not tell her, however, that a plane flew over Busch Stadium pulling a banner that said THE METS ARE POND SCUM.

At the age of eleven, Lori already knows The Game. She knows that the Mets are not pond scum but whipped cream, that a safety squeeze is not a way to hold a hand grenade, that Astroturf belongs in a colorful parking lot, and that Mookie Wilson has class and the Cardinals have none. Why, she knew at nine that 1-and-2 is a pitcher's pitch, that there are many fine saliva substitutes for making a spitball, and that a high five is not a basketball team on cocaine.

Beneath a huge picture of Mookie, Lori now is turning restlessly in her sleep. She is good at going to her left in bed, so I center her, hoping she will be able to go to her left just as well when she tries out for shortstop on her school softball team. I have been helping her practice fielding grounders; and every one she misses makes her laugh and cry "Billy Buckner!" in ironic tribute to the Boston first baseman who was a spectator for Mookie's World Series grounder, giving us a victory I cherish the way I cherish Bobby Thompson's home run. As part of a history lesson, I have been trying to teach Lori the old Giants' alma mater, "We're Calling All Fans," but she is more moved by the Mets' video and the songs of the Monkees.

The tune in my head now changes from the Giants' theme to the Monkees' "O how I wish tomorrow would never come," which is *my* theme. I fear tomorrow, and I fear all the parts of today that make me want to hide, and I ask myself again: *is* there anyplace to hide from terror and time?

Suddenly, I know: I know the one place where I always have felt safe and happy and young, especially now that Lori is there with me. Baseball. *Baseball* is a loveliness that lasts. Looking at a photo of Lori in her Mets uniform shirt, a photo taken the year she fell in love with baseball, I think with profound contentment about this fan of eleven and her father of fifty-four, and then I think about the sweetness of all my years with The Game.

When I was eleven . . .

2
The One-Sewer Man
and the .700 Girl

Lori and I
Discover The Game

"*H*indu! Hindu!" was the cry that I heard as I came out into the street, but I didn't look for a man with a snake. I looked at the boys who were playing stickball in front of the house where I had just moved and I saw the reason for the cry: one of the bases was driving away.

"It woulda been *fair!*" said a thin boy with glasses as he ran to the spot the car had left and then lunged at it with the carpet-sweeper handle that was his bat. "The fender was right *here!* Goddammit, *fair ball!*"

"You're outa your mind, Morey," said a thin, muscular boy who was standing on the piece of Consolidated Edison called second base.

"Freddie's right," said a beefy blond boy. "His two eyes are better'n your four."

"What can *you* see, Howie, with your head so far up your ass?"

"Okay, *okay*," said Freddie, raising his mighty right arm. "It's a Hindu and we're takin' it over. Back o' the Chevy is the new first."

Having issued the last word, Freddie bounced the pink rubber ball a couple of times, while I watched with wonder at how a spaldeen jumped up off the street with a life of its own; and then he prepared to pitch to Morey, who was standing again at home manhole with his bat cocked above his mastoid scar and his feet pressed together like Stan Musial's.

"Come on, Morey!" cried a boy who was sitting on a Hudson just behind home. "Send it three sewers, babe!"

"Send him *into* the sewer!" cried the beefy boy from his fielding position in the power alley near the Chinese laundry. "No hitter, Freddie, no hitter!"

About thirty feet above these sporting reflections, a woman with hair like steel wool and a flowered bathrobe leaned from a brownstone windowsill and cried, "Shut up, you noisy bums! Shut up that noise or I call the cops and they call your fathers if you *got* any!"

Across the street, another woman leaned from a high brick bleacher seat and sent a more constructive suggestion to one of the players:

"Beanie, don't get *killed*! You watch those cars, you *hear*?"

With a look of filial disgust, the boy on the Hudson looked upward and said, "F' Crissake, Ma, you see me gettin' killed?"

"Isn't that beautiful?" said an on-deck hitter in horn-rimmed glasses to Beanie. "She wants you back."

As I watched these boys playing stickball on that April morning in 1944, I was dreaming of hitting a drive all the way to the far side of Broadway, past the warning track where the trolley ran, past the grandmothers on mid-Broadway benches who watched centerfielders chase balls headed for another neighborhood. I was dreaming of getting into The Game on a diamond that was the long rectangle of a Manhattan side street: early

Astroturf with manholes, where first and third were fenders that could not have been Mitsubishis because Japanese planes never parked on that street.

But before I could hit that Broadway blast, before I could send a spaldeen bouncing toward the five-and-ten from where it had come, I would have to join one of the teams; and I was so afraid to introduce myself to these boys that my heart was hammering at the spot where my chest should have been. I was certain they would not like me or believe I was almost twelve. At four feet nine and a weight that belonged on a postal scale, I could have passed for eight. I was going to have my twelfth birthday next month; but I saw no point in being twelve until someone took me for eleven.

If I could manage to enter this game, I would begin my baseball career the way that Lori would begin hers exactly forty years later at the age of eight: in an asphalt version of baseball that used a rubber ball— mine a spaldeen and hers more fitting for seals in a circus. In the fall of 1984, in a public school playground in Princeton, New Jersey, Lori broke into second-grade kickball with a batting average of about .700, consistently kicking extra-base hits through defenses that looked like large exercise classes. With a dozen or more players on each team, kickball presented a grandly cluttered defense against each batter. There was, for example, no such thing as a single in the hole because the hole contained five or six shortstops, none of whom could go to his left because another shortstop was blocking his way. However, the glory of baseball is such that the game is playground proof: even this version to which Lori was introduced at eight, a game that looked like a subway platform, enchanted her at once.

As a hitter, Lori quickly developed the ability to guess right on every pitch, perhaps because every pitch was the same: a straight roller down the middle, a hanging beachball. Every pitch was a mistake, but it was hard for a pitcher to do much with a kickball except roll a fat one or deflate it. Nevertheless, even though ERAs were invariably in double figures, and even though the average fielder was skilled at bouncing the ball off the cutoff man, Lori's first inside-the-park home run was so intoxicating to her that she ran home from school almost as fast to share it with me. She had found a pitch that was just her shoe size and driven it into a crowd of center-fielders; and then she started running with the speed that had been delighting me since she was six. As she was dashing for third, one of the fielders played the carom off a friend and tried to hit her with the ball, a throw that would have tested Willie Mays, but she pirouetted away; and then she eluded another fielder who chased her home with the ball.

"It was so *great*, Daddy!" she told me. "They threw it at me and they chased me with it, but I got all the way to home base!"

"That's terrific, honey; I'm really proud of you," I said. "Do they ever try tagging people at the bases?"

"Why would they do *that*?"

"It's a crazy way baseball is played sometimes. They even have *two*-man rundowns."

"Daddy, I *love* baseball."

"And you'll love it even more when you play it."

A few days later at school, Lori had a new triumph as heady as the hit that had dared those fielders to follow the bouncing ball. In the bottom of the third inning, she was standing in centerfield, taking a little sun, when the kicker launched a fly that came directly at her. She had never before caught a fly, for the ball was the size of her chest and too big a missile to be intercepted by her; but suddenly, she found her arms around it and there it stopped, incredulously embraced by a player cuter than Bill Veeck's midget.

And then she heard the cheers.

"Hey, what a catch!"

"Way to go, little Lori!"

"Did you see Lori *catch* it?"

However, when she reported this triumph to me after school, its splendor was tarnished by the references to her size.

"They keep calling me little Lori," she said with a curl of her lower lip.

"*You'll* grow, honey," I told her. "*I* did—about half a foot when I was sixteen. I was *always* the smallest one in the game, and the rotten way I played had *nothing* to do with my size."

"I bet you weren't rotten," she said, letting a smile break through. "You're just saying that."

"I was a *little* rotten. I definitely wasn't as good as *you.*"

Her lower lip unrolled again. "Well, I still don't like being little."

"But size doesn't mean a *thing* in baseball. Pee Wee Reese—a Hall of Famer—was called The Little Colonel and Lloyd Waner was called Little Poison and Wee Willie Keeler was . . . Wee Willie; he's the one who said, 'Hit 'em where they ain't.' Of course, you can't do that in kickball. By the way, short players also walk a lot."

"What's a walk?"

"Four balls and then you go to first base. You'll see when you start playing real baseball and the game doesn't look like a windy beach."

If I could get into that game on a side street in 1944, I would be under more pressure than Lori was in the playground forty years later, not only because I was small for a game that was all bigger boys but also because a spaldeen was much harder to hit with a thin stick than a fat rolling ball was with a foot. What comfort I felt every time I saw one of the boys strike out, for striking out was something I was sure I could do.

"Man, did that *drop*," said Beanie, admiring one of Freddie's strikeout pitches, while I continued to watch with yearning from the sidewalk in front of the Club 78.

"*Anybody* can make a spaldeen drop," said Morey, walking away from the plate in disgust. "That's what it *does*."

"You'd need two more eyes to hit a watermelon," said Freddie with a cocky grin as his team came in to bat. "All you Japanese are finished now."

"Up yours with gauze," said Morey, who did look a little Japanese, but who had the guts of John Wayne to say such a line to the strongest boy on the block, even though it seemed to me that rising gauze would not have bothered Freddie.

In the following inning, Freddie led off for his team and he stood at the plate like DiMaggio: his feet far apart, his head motionless, and his bat defiantly high. His fly was open too, but all the rest of him was Yankee Clipper. The first pitch to him from the boy with horn-rimmed glasses was a nothing ball down the middle,

26

but Freddie let it go by to a silver-haired man in a purple shirt, who was the catcher for both teams.

"That had three sewers written all over it," the catcher told Freddie, and then he called to the pitcher, "Sydney, you better put more than your fingers on the next one or it's Broadway blast."

"You're supposed to be *neuter*, Harry," cried Beanie from the field.

And then it came: one of the sweetest sounds I knew, a sound as sweet as the bells of the Good Humor man or my mother singing "Blueberry Hill." It was the pop of a stick redirecting a spaldeen. Freddie had connected with the next pitch and the ball had become a pink blur flying toward the building that held the left-field seats. It hit a high ledge and ricocheted toward Morey, who was drifting around while looking skyward like an air-raid warden in a night attack. He probably wanted to play the carom the way Furillo played it at Ebbets Field; but Morey's play was harder, for Furillo never had baby carriages coming from the bullpen. While Morey's mother cried from her fourth-floor seat, "Maurice, watch the *cars*!" her daring darling just missed a parked Plymouth and instead backed into a passing baby carriage, giving the child a chance to do some traveling on his own.

Meanwhile, Freddie was jubilantly circling the bases in the city boy's ellipses, from fender to manhole to fender to manhole, while the ball bounced west across Broadway and his team wildly cheered. It was a home run that left me in awe, for it had gone almost three sewers on the fly, plus a major intersection on the bounce. When Morey's mother saw him chasing the ball through a red Broadway light, she almost took the fast way down to the street; but I knew that he would slip safely through because a city boy could always sidestep cars like a matador.

A few seconds after this magnificent hit, while Morey was making the long trek back with the spaldeen after its journey toward New Jersey, a sharp splat startled me and I turned to see the boys dancing back from the spot where the woman with steel-wool hair had just dumped a pail of water from her window.

"You lousy bums!" she cried. "People trying to *sleep*! I call the cops!"

As the game stopped for this rain delay, Freddie looked up at the woman and cried, "Why dontcha sleep at *night* like everyone *else*, you old Nazi bitch!" His tongue was as splendid as his bat.

"Go soak your *own* head," Sydney said, which sounded even better to me.

What wonderful lousy bums these were! And what a wonderful game!

All the while I was waiting to play on that day in '44, I was tossing my own new spaldeen to myself the way that Lori loves to toss anything from a tennis ball to a tangerine. In fact, dinner at our house sometimes looks like "This Week in Baseball," for Lori will suddenly grab a baked potato, cock her arm, and say, "I'm Darryl, you're HoJo, let's get 'im at third!" More than once, I have given new meaning to the hot corner by applying a tag with a yam to a runner sliding toward our sink, while my wife, Judy, watched and wondered if my parents were first cousins. Lori also plays with dolls, just like girls who are not Darryl, but her quick little hands are most attracted to throwable and semithrowable spheres. I have tried to make her understand that even Johnny Bench could never have caught a man stealing with a green pepper; but once a child has discovered the infinite pleasure of throwing a ball, be it horsehide, rubber, or vegetable, that child is as happily addicted as Tommy John, who said, "The part I'll miss most is the best part: throwing the baseball." The Game begins with the ball, which demands to be thrown, as Lori well knows: she has been in love with the ball since she was seven and now throws everything but soft-boiled eggs. Hard-boiled eggs, of course, can nicely hit a cutoff man.

After dinner, if the weather is warm, we go outside the house to practice her fielding with a tennis ball or hardball, or to practice her hitting with a Wiffle ball, or to practice her pitching with them all. Because she wants to play second or short on her school softball team, I work hard with her, delighted that she did not inherit my only flaw as an infielder: a fear of ground balls. Lori fields aggressively, making her throw with a quick release whether or not she has the ball.

"Don't start throwing before you've really got it," I tell her.

"*Look*, Dad," she cries. "I can throw *sidearm* too. Watch me do sidearm *pitching*."

"There are no shortstops who also pitch."

"I'll be the first."

"Honey, sidearmers can be wild. You remember what I told you about Carl Mays?"

"The pitcher who killed a guy. But everyone has helmets now, so not so many guys get killed."

"Right. The death toll is way down, especially in the National League."

"Dad, was Carl Mays Willie's father?"

"Probably not; he was white."

"Jackie Robinson was the first black player in the whole major leagues, right?"

"He certainly was."

"Well, I'm going to be the first woman."

"You know, I think you just might."

"I'm learning to switch-hit too, just like Mookie."

"Yes, what a jump Mookie gets. You know, hitting left-handed saves you two steps to first."

"I wonder who the fastest woman running to first ever was."

"There are probably no records."

"I don't care; let's look it up."

One evening, we had infield practice with a spaldeen in the hall of our house the way I had played in the hall of my boyhood apartment overlooking the stickball field. I threw her hard grounders, line drives, and short hops that sometimes bounced through to the piano, where she also had good hands, where I loved to hear her play minuets; and at times I wondered if I should have been encouraging her to play more Bach than second base, for I knew of no sustained careers in both baseball and music. Darryl Strawberry had made a record, but it was the musical equivalent of Chopin playing short.

Our infield practice was ended by a call to dinner, at which no rolls began double plays; but when we had finished eating and Lori was leading me to her room to review either some homework or George Vecsey's column, she suddenly picked up a tennis ball, whirled around, and cried, "Terry Leach against Jack Clark!"

Most of the time when Lori pitched, she stood erect facing third, pumped slowly with a solemn look, came to a full stop, and then delivered; but this time the game situation—runners on the scatter rugs, the dangerous Clark at bat in the foyer—called for a sidearm quick pitch; and like many sidearmers, especially the ones who pitch immediately after a meal, Lori was wild. The ball flew past me, but it did not fly past an antique china bowl on a coffee table nearby—the kind of bull's-eye that won a stuffed animal at an amusement park.

Watching us pick up the pieces of this bowl from the living-room floor, Judy said, "It was crazy of me to put it on a ball field. I should have put it on the lawn."

"Look, it could have happened to *anyone* throwing a ball through the room," I said.

"Yes, that's an excellent point. And clearly I can't punish her because I'd have to punish you too. But can't the two of you *please* try to respect something of value?"

We do respect something of value, I thought. *We respect baseball.*

"Hey, if I get another guy, can I play?" I said to the boys with more courage than I thought I had.

"Where do you see another guy?" said Freddie.

"What about him?" I said, pointing to the silver-haired man in the purple shirt.

"Harry only plays if the other team has a bookie too."

"The eight of us have been living here for about forty years," Morey said. "You shoulda come then."

"It would *still* be an odd number, you schmuck," said Sydney. "If we'd've let him play *then*, why not let him play *now*? Freddie can equal two guys."

"Okay, look," said Freddie, pointing his mighty bat at me. "You can play with them. My team doesn't need any more."

"Hey, *thanks*!" I said, too stupid to know I had just been told I was meaningless.

"You play deep center," Morey told me.

"How deep?" I said.

"Across the street," he said with a laugh that made me want to punch his unusual face. He did look like a Japanese with red hair, and I pictured John Wayne shooting him with a cry of "Take *that*, you yellow red!" or maybe, "Take *that*, you red-headed yellow!"

"Cut the shit, Morey," said Freddie. "He stays on *this* side of Broadway."

"Gee, thanks," I told Freddie, a little too grateful for being allowed to play a position that was in the neighborhood.

Moments later, I nervously took my place at the manhole just before Broadway and looked up to study the houses on both sides of the street to see if I could predict the caroms of drives that might be coming to me. I could not, of course, predict a thing, except that I had a good chance of falling into one of the five or six cellars that lay at the bottom of steep stone steps on both the left- and right-field sidewalks. I wondered if anyone would notice if I suddenly disappeared.

As a boy named Howie came to bat, I spread my legs, bent my knees a bit, and peered hard toward the distant home plate the way I presumed real outfielders did. I might not have been able to detect a spaldeen flying out to me, but at least I would see any automobile that crossed the field from the Amsterdam Avenue end because the field was a one-way street. In fact, my mother need not have worried about my playing deep center-field because four other boys would have had to be run down before my turn arrived. What my mother and I did not know was that police cars could come in either direction; and so, the one that suddenly stopped beside me caught our boys in a sneak attack that was hardly the American way being fought for by other boys on other fields.

"Okay, let's have the stick," said one of the cops.

Moving with the reflexes that made him King of the West Side Sewers, Freddie had already thrown the stick into the bushes of the third-base building, while his fellow sportsmen struck the casual poses of curbside conversationalists and Harry quickly began to improve his mind with the *Daily News*.

"You!" cried the other cop to Freddie. "Get that stick and bring it here!"

"What's the charge, Officer?" I said.

"A racket that's keeping people from sleeping," he replied while the players slowly came to the car, with Freddie dragging the bat as if he were walking a Basset hound.

"But the only people who should be sleeping now are in *China*," I said, and some of the boys laughed.

"What're you, a comical midget?" said the first cop.

"No, it's just that people usually sleep at *night*—except on New Year's Eve."

"Okay, wise guy," he said, pulling out his pad, "I'm takin' *your* name first—for the Juvenile Bureau."

"He's new around here," said the other cop, "but the rest of 'em know damn well that stickball belongs in the park."

"But it's against the *law* to play on the grass," I said.

The first cop looked at me with a little smile of disgust. "Okay, midget, let's have your name."

"Joseph Dzhugashvili," I said, trying not to laugh.

"Joseph *what*?"

"Dzhu-gash-vili. Believe me, I'd rather be Mel Ott."

"Don't be smart, Joseph; just give it to me slow," he said, and slowly I gave him Stalin's old name.

Following my lead, the eight other boys then gave names that they felt were more fitting for the occasion than their own. After he had finished his list of fictional characters, the first cop said, "One last chance, that's what I'm givin' ya. I'm gonna letcha keep the stick this time, but the next complaint we get about this goddam game, we're takin' more than just your names."

As the cops drove off, Freddie turned to me and said, "And I thought *Sydney* had a mouth. Ralphie, that was *great*."

"Thanks," I said, feeling almost as good as if I had hit for a couple of sewers.

"Yeah, giving that phony Italian name, that was terrific," Howie told me.

"It's not Italian. It's Stalin's real name."

"No kiddin'," said Morey. "I shoulda given 'em Schicklgruber instead of Francis Flynn."

"Well, at least you guys gave 'em phony names too," I said.

"Phony for us but real for our elevator men," Freddie replied.

And then the nine of us laughingly spread out on the field to continue the happiest crime I knew.

In the bottom of the seventh inning, while I was playing my profoundly deep centerfield, Freddie connected again but with too much uppercut and hit a fly so high that I lost sight of it for a second or two; and then, trying to get under the ball as it drifted toward a building, I staggered backward across the sidewalk and through the open door of a Chinese laundry to become the first man in stickball history ever to chase a fly indoors. When the laundryman asked me for my ticket, I was reminded once again that my sporting destiny might not be chock-full of glory. I knew that even when he was twelve, DiMaggio always went for the ball and never his boxer shorts.

3
Giants and Pygmies

We Start to Love the National League

*T*he following month, a few days after my twelfth birthday, I left the sewers of that street for the heights of a place called Coogan's Bluff to see my first game of professional baseball: the New York Giants against the Chicago Cubs. Lori's Mets were born in these Polo Grounds in 1962, five years after the Giants left, but those early Mets were clearly the illegitimate sons of the poignant team that I grew to love as much as Lori has grown to love hers. From the Giants to the Mets: the torch had been passed—and dropped; but what else could the '62 Mets do with a torch passed by a team that for seventeen years had turned my heart into a yo-yo?

I discovered the tragicomedy of the Polo Grounds on a May afternoon in 1945, when my grandfather took me to a game that was won with a ninth-inning home run by an enormous catcher who had the grace of a drugged elephant, a nose that left the strike zone in shadow, and a uniform that should have been sheltering sleeping Arabs.

"That's The Schnozz," said Gramp, who had been

laughing and crying at the Giants even before Merkle forgot to touch second.

As lovable as Marvelous Marv Throneberry, The Schnozz, also known as Ernie Lombardi, was an inert giant of a Giant, who stood at the plate with his bat on his shoulder like a man with a fishing pole waiting for a streetcar. But suddenly his wrists—his only moving parts—would whip the bat into the ball and send it flying so fast that it could have killed the shortstop, even though he was playing in left field.

The first time The Schnozz came to bat, my grandfather said, "He's the slowest man you've ever seen, Ralphie. He walks out his hits. If it isn't a triple, he won't make first."

I was enjoying my grandfather's little joke until The Schnozz, one of The Game's greatest hitters, lined a fastball off the left-field wall and was thrown out at first on a double. In the last of the ninth, he hit a drive just as hard but a few feet higher and it landed in the seats. When it took him about a minute to circle the bases, I cheered and laughed and knew that this was my team.

The one-minute home run was hardly the only appeal on the '45 Giants, one of the two National League teams in New York at that time. Another giant of a Giant was the first baseman, Johnny "Big Jawn" Mize, whose cheeks bulged with tobacco as he stood poised to pounce on anything hit directly at him; and I also liked to watch the bulging muscles in his arms when he was at bat. Comparative anatomy at the Polo Grounds was fun: The Schnozz's nose, Big Jawn's arms, and the right leg of the little right fielder, Mel Ott. Just before he swung his bat, Ott swung his right leg into the air, as if allowing a small animal to go by; and then he regained enough balance to do something pleasant with the ball.

On that May day, both Ott and Big Jawn pulled soft flies down the right-field line. Both times, the Cub first baseman backed up hopefully, but the balls fell just beyond him for home runs.

"That's China," said Gramp, pointing to the corner of the right-field wall, where the sign said 257; and then he pointed to the centerfield clubhouse, where the sign said 483. "And that's Siberia."

This ball park was as entertaining as the Giants themselves. Some right-handed hitters would try to hold off on a pitch, only to find that they had dropped a homer into the inscrutable East, while others would drive a fastball four hundred feet, only to find the centerfielder moving in for it.

"To hit well here," Gramp told me, "your timing has to be off."

"Ott's timing is off best of all, isn't it?" I said.

"Yes, he's King of China, all right; but I'm afraid some of his shots wouldn't be homers in real ball parks. He belongs right here, or Little League."

If the right-field stands were China, those in left had to be Japan. Although just twenty-two feet deeper, they were sufficiently nearby to make a utility infielder feel like Hank Greenberg. Their thick, jutting scoreboard made homers of flies that fell to the left fielder after only minor deflections.

"Damn! Another brusher!" said Gramp, while an equally disgusted Giant watched a fly caress the scoreboard before dropping to him. The following inning, Phil Cavarretta hit the scoreboard on a pitch that Gramp suspected he had been trying to take.

After that game with the Cubs, the Giants went on to win twenty-five of the next thirty-two. As June began, they were in first place by seven games.

"I sure picked the right team," I told Gramp. "We'll clinch the pennant by the Fourth of July."

"That's when our season usually ends," he replied. "Ralphie, you still don't know what it means to be a Giant fan."

His pessimism bewildered me; and I was even more bewildered a few weeks later: our team collapsed and he seemed fulfilled.

"That's more like it," he said after the Giants had fallen to fifth, where they finished. "I knew they could do it."

"But Gramp," I said, "if you love the Giants so much, why don't you pull for them to stay on top?"

He smiled sadly. "You can love a sick cat and still not expect him to catch any mice. *Now* you know what it means to be a Giant fan: no matter how big our lead, we can always find a way to blow it."

He was the first Zen Giants fan, for his rooting was the sound of one hand clapping.

A few days later, I understood this natural law he had given to me. In the bottom of the ninth at St. Louis, a Cardinal hitter named Johnny Hopp faced our pitcher, Bill Voiselle, with the winning run on base. Ahead 0-and-2, Voiselle threw a pitch down the middle in a try for strike three, and he would have had it but for Hopp's triple.

"That's a basic rule for pitchers," Gramp told me. "Never throw three straight strikes. Of course, the boys don't have much trouble obeying it these days."

The next Sunday, the Giants returned me to dismay by losing both ends of a doubleheader in extra innings.

"What's *wrong* with us?" I asked Gramp.

"We forgot to replace Hubbell and Schumacher," he said. "Our pitchers should be pitching batting practice."

"They *are*," I said and we both laughed.

"But the good thing is we never blow a game the same way twice. Baseball is wonderful, Ralphie, even for Giants fans. So many possibilities."

The following year, the Giants explored still a new one: emigration. Seven of them left not only the team but the country. Sal Maglie and six others fled to the Mexican League, where they knew they would play for a better team. Those who had not escaped seemed so ashamed of the breakout that they spent the rest of the season hiding in eighth place.

"Don't worry," said Gramp, "they had the stuff to finish last even if those guys hadn't gone to Mexico."

And so, in my second season as a Giant fan, the part of my team that played above the Rio Grande had sunk to the cellar; but I still found delight in watching them, even though it seemed unlikely to be able to find delight in despair. No matter what anguish the Giants induced, and they induced creatively in the ninth inning, they were still playing The Game.

"Daddy," said Lori as we walked toward the den of our house to see the Mets, "it's stupid not to have the pitcher bat, right?"

"Absolutely," I replied. "It kills a lot of the strategy. It's like tennis with three serves."

"How many are you supposed to get?"

I smiled at the face beneath the Mets cap. "I'll teach you tennis next."

"But baseball is better, right?"

"For tennis you need only two people."

"Baseball *too:* just *us.* Daddy, you gotta see me switch-hit. I'm getting ready for the team at school. Won't it be great? A switch-hitter who runs like Mookie!"

"You don't have to switch-hit yet. Twelve-year-olds can't throw curves, especially with a softball."

"I'll bet my *Bubble Baby* could when he was twelve. Did you see the story about his great sense of humor?"

"All those funny fires he starts?"

"Yeah, it's on my closet."

"So that's where the sports section went."

"Hey, wouldn't it be great if you could switch-*pitch*? Throw with either *hand.*"

"I think there are pitchers in the American League who are throwing with the wrong hand."

Moments later, we reached our television set, where Lori's grandfather, Milton, was watching a game. Milton was an honorable man, but he did have one character flaw: he liked the Yankees.

"Grampa!" cried Lori when she saw the pin-striped aliens on the screen. "We don't want to watch the stinking Yankees!"

"Don't use language like that, Lori," he said.

"Right," I told her. "Don't say Yankees."

"But Grampa, we're only four games *out* and we're *hitting* again! Dwight is back and Lee is awesome and Darryl and HoJo *both* have almost thirty home runs!"

"Just let Grampa watch a couple of innings," I said, "and then we'll turn to baseball."

Lori's lower lip curled out, the way it did whenever HoJo made an error or Bubble Baby was taken deep or the sports section talked about trading Mookie; and in a fearful voice, she said, "Daddy, do I *have* to watch the DH?"

"We'll pretend it's a cartoon," I told her. "DH stands for . . . for . . . *Daffy Hardball*."

"No, for *Dopey* . . . *Dopey* . . ."

"Dopey Hybridization," I said, and she laughed as if she understood the word; but then her lip suddenly recurled.

"We might be missing my *Bubble* Baby pitching."

"I hope not. That would mean we're in trouble."

"Ralph," said Milt as his beloved stinking Yankees took the field, "why do you tell her such things about the American League?"

"Milt," I said with soft solemnity, "there are three absolutes in life that a father has to teach his daughter if he is to raise her properly: Bach is the greatest composer, love is the only foundation for marriage, and the American League is a bore."

"*Yeah*, Grampa," said Lori, "you don't have any pitchers like Dwight or Mike Scott or Fernando or . . . or . . . *tell* him, Daddy."

"Milt, ask Bobby Murcer what happened when he went from the Yankees to the Giants. Ask Lance Parrish which league has better pitching."

"Didn't he beat us with a homer last week?" Lori said.

"Let's go outside till Grampa switches," I replied, and I led her out of the den and toward our backyard. On the way, we picked up our three different balls: a tennis ball, a Wiffle ball, and a softball the size of a hardball. However, before any one of them went into play, my own fielding practice began—fielding Lori's never-ending questions about The Game:

"Why is a split-finger fastball so hard to hit?"

"When does a relief pitcher win the game?"

"Who's faster: Lenny or Mookie?"

"Wanna see me spit like Whitey Herzog?"

"Who's a better fielder: Lenny or Mookie?"

"Who was the greatest pitcher ever?"

"Who's cuter: Lenny or Mookie?"

"How can Gary bat cleanup with a .236 average?"

"Why doesn't Kevin ever smile?"

"Wanna see me shuffle my hips like Tim's?"

"Are my bubbles as big as Roger's?"

There was just one question I could not answer, the one that had stumped me often before:

"Daddy, what are we going to do when baseball season is over and dumb football starts?"

"Well, honey . . ." I said with a little chill, "baseball is never really *over* when it's over."

"Yogi Berra said that, right?"

"Either Yogi Berra or Justice Holmes. The point is we have our Mets videos and our baseball books . . . and the memories of the games we saw at Shea and on TV . . . and *we* can keep playing till the snow falls—then *too;* in fact, you can work on your split-finger *snowball.*"

In spite of my upbeat chatter, Lori's thought of no baseball for six months had made my heart suddenly sink; and for a moment, I wondered if she and I should start spending our winters in Venezuela. Lori had other loves, but even her pet was in the shadow of The Game. She had called her hamster Mookie, ignoring my suggestion that a more fitting name for a baseball rodent would have been Walter O'Malley.

"Daddy," she said as we stood in the yard, "you said nobody steals home anymore, right?"

"Right; too easy to get hurt by the catcher. It's a better play for football."

"Well, I figured out a way—if there's a guy on first too. That guy steals second and the catcher throws down there, and then the guy on third sneaks home while nobody's paying attention."

Filled with pride to have a daughter who looked like a Botticelli and thought like Branch Rickey, I dropped my arms around her and gave her a hug.

"You're a *genius!*" I cried through a mouthful of hair. "That's *exactly* the way the pros have tried it!"

She flexed her lower lip again. "You mean somebody thought of it first?"

"Honey, you're not the *only* person who knows baseball. It's catching on nicely all over the country."

"But wasn't it great the way I knew that HoJo would cream that three-and-one pitch because he had to get a fastball and that's his cream pitch."

"Absolutely. You're ready for graduate school."

Was it wise for a father to keep telling his daughter that she was wonderful? Was my response to Lori more fitting for one of the Magi? But the world would be knocking her down soon enough, I thought, so why not build her confidence? My own father had often told me that I was the greatest man in the world, confusing me with Albert Schweitzer but adding a couple of feet to my height.

"Now, come on, genius," I said, "let's play ball. Voiselle pitching to Mookie."

In the early days of 1947, I was filled with more hope than belonged in any Giant fan, for the spring-training stories spoke of a magnificent rookie from Hondo, Texas, who had the power of Babe Ruth. Called The Hondo Hurricane, Clint Hartung not only could hit a ball five hundred feet but he also could pitch.

"That's the one thing we've needed," said Gramp. "A pitcher who can hit five hundred feet."

When The Hondo Hurricane finally blew into the Polo Grounds, our manager, Mel Ott, was so overwhelmed by Hondo's all-purpose splendor that he did not know where to play him. After a few weeks of the season, however, it did not matter where Hondo played because it turned out that he was equally inept at several positions. And to complement his versatile rottenness in the field, he wasted no time in mounting a pursuit of the National League strikeout record. He could, of course, produce five-hundred-foot drives, but only if you let him pitch.

Fortunately, our real hitters made up for the wind of the Hurricane's bat: Big Jawn, Bill Rigney, Sid Gordon, Walker Cooper, Willard Marshall, and Bobby Thomson attacked both sides of the Orient for 221 home runs, a major-league record. Even more impressive was the achievement of hitting 221 home runs and finishing fourth.

What did the Giants need? The answer was clear: a song. Since incessant home runs merely kept them out of fifth place, the missing ingredient had to be music; and now mine became the only team in the majors to have an anthem. How proudly I sang:

> *"We're calling all fans,*
> *All you Giant ball fans.*
> *Come see the home team*

Going places 'round the bases.
Cheer for your fav'rites
Out at Coogan's Bluff.
You'll see those Polo Grounders
Do their stuff."

In 1948, although stirred by this song, the Giants continued to do their stuff. They needed more than cheap home runs and an alma mater to leave the second division, they needed a spark plug. In July, they got one: owner Horace Stoneham fired Mel Ott and hired the considerably louder Leo Durocher. Stoneham also moved the equally noisy Frankie Frisch, a great Giant infielder of the past, from the radio booth to the coaching box. At third base, Frisch's rooting for the Giants no longer annoyed those listeners who occasionally wanted to know what the visiting team was doing.

In the radio booth, Frisch had told of our games in a style that could only be called stream of semiconsciousness. Uniquely blending nostalgia and hysteria, he kept swinging between memory ("Ah, The Old Flash remembers the day when . . .") and panic ("There's a smash down to—oh, a *great*—but it's *wild* and—oh, look at *that*! But the run's gonna—what a fantastic play! Just like the last game of that Series when—but let's recap it first"). While the Old Flash reminisced about the recent action on the field, adding such color as the names of the players, the visiting team scored a few more runs, moving him to moan, "Oh, those bases on balls will kill you every time."

Our pitchers would have given still more bases on balls had they not been hit so hard. Because of such pitching, even The Old Flash and Leo the Lip could not

49

inspire us to leave fifth place; and the following year, we remained in fifth, but with so much spirit that Leo was suspended from baseball for hitting a fan. The Giants had always known how to hit.

After this humiliation of our manager, I felt that things could get no worse; but for the Giants, things always could. Although Leo was pardoned by the commissioner, two weeks later Sid Gordon, Buddy Kerr, and Willard Marshall were traded to the Braves for Alvin Dark and Eddie Stanky. It was my blackest day. Gramp and I loved Sid Gordon and not merely because he was Jewish; we loved many Gentile players too.

Strangely enough, however, this trade made Gramp uncharacteristically optimistic.

"Here's the thing about Stanky," he said. "He can't really hit or field, but he's short and walks a lot. And he fights like Leo."

"So now we've got *two* thugs," I said. "Does Dark have a record too?"

"No, but he pulls the ball down the line. He can hit almost three hundred feet and he always pulls. More Polo Grounds power, Ralphie. More homers made in Japan."

We did not know, of course, about a different kind of power—and glory—that were on their way in the form of a player who rated not "We're Calling All Fans" but *The Messiah*. Just a long look at Willie Mays told us that here was the greatest player who ever lived. It would not be easy to lose with a man who played in his own stratosphere.

"I'm afraid it looks good," said Gramp one day when Willie stole home right after catching a ball with his bare right hand. "I wonder if we still can blow it."

We could not: with Willie playing all three outfield positions at once, blowing it was beyond our power now. Instead, the Dodgers borrowed our tradition. Thirteen games ahead of us on August 12, they then swooned their way to that playoff in which Bobby Thomson sent an earthquake to Japan, twenty feet over Andy Pafko's head.

We lost the World Series to the Yankees, and we won no pennant the following year, for on May 29 our entire team was drafted: Willie went into the army. Six months later, I left Gramp to enter this army too, savoring the thought that Willie and I were now in the same uniform. I pictured us together on a battlefield in Korea. Suddenly, a hand grenade was coming at us through the air.

All yours, Willie! I cried, knowing that after the catch, his throw would nail a half dozen North Koreans in their dugout.

In the spring of 1954, displaying a sense of symmetry, the gods sent this Giant fan to Japan at precisely the moment they sent Willie back to the other Japan of Coogan's Bluff. And then, in early October, at five o'clock one morning, I was putting on fatigues in a barracks at Camp Zama, while on my bed a shortwave radio's inconstant voice was describing Willie's celestial catch of a four-hundred-eighty-foot drive by Cleveland's Vic Wertz in the first game of the World Series. On a sprint toward the centerfield clubhouse, with his back to the ball, Willie had taken the heart out of Cleveland with the kind of catch that only wide receivers made.

Moments later, as I double-timed from the barracks into a cold, dark Japanese morning, I was the only soldier smiling. And I knew that six thousand miles away, Gramp was smiling too and thinking, *We haven't won a World Series since the year Ralphie was born.*

"Daddy, was Willie Mays really the greatest player who ever lived?" said Lori after seeing a tape about Willie that she had given to me for Father's Day.

"Leo the Lip says so," I replied.

"Can he do *this* with his lip?"

"You have to compete with everyone, don't you? Even a man of eighty. What an *American* you are."

"Did you ever meet Leo the Lip?"

"I interviewed him once, and he said there are only five things a player can do. Go ahead, name them."

"Hit, field, run . . . spit—there's only *three*."

"No, it's hit for average, hit for power, field, throw, and run."

"Well, I knew a *lot* of them."

"Right, three out of five; that's an F."

"Ask me how many steals and home runs Darryl and HoJo have."

"Save it for the SATs. Anyway, Leo said that Willie was the only player who ever did all five perfectly. Ruth and DiMaggio were no big threats to steal, and even Joe never made the catches Willie did. Sometimes when Willie was running top speed to his right, he caught the ball *bare-handed*."

"*I* can do that."

"It wasn't a spaldeen. Leo used to say, 'If the ball stays in the park, Willie'll get it.' Remember the other day when Mookie and Darryl ran into each other?"

"It wasn't *Mookie's* fault," said Lori.

"And it wasn't the first time: they've perfected that

play. Well, Willie never ran into anyone because the other fielders just got out of his way. Willie always made me think of the greatest thing about baseball. Remember what it is?"

"Don't tell me, *I'll* get it."

While she thought, I gazed at her: my third daughter, my final miracle, who was growing up with big stunning eyes and a brain that already had found a way to steal home. I knew well that accident was the dominant law of life; but in a world of accidents, most of them grim, the cosmic dice roll again had given me the best thing a man could have: someone to show me the endless manifestations that can be taken by love.

"The greatest thing about baseball is watching Mookie play," she said.

"No," I told her, "the greatest thing is in every game you see something you've never seen before."

"I was close."

"Like that guy on the Padres who stopped running to first and ran back to home when Keith got the throw down the line. Wasn't that hilarious?"

"Yes, but we had the same *thing* in a game at school. This dopey kid turned around and started back to home, so we had to throw him *out* at home."

"Which doesn't happen so often on a grounder to the pitcher," I said through my laughter. "Your catcher made baseball *history:* a putout of a runner coming from *first.* I wonder if baseball would be even better if they played it clockwise."

For a few minutes, we reminisced about some of the crazy plays we had seen, in her schoolyard, in our backyard, and at Shea, and our stories took my mind off the sadness I had just felt watching Willie Mays retire again.

When his career ended at Shea on that day in 1973, I had thought that my boyhood had ended too. Ten years later, a second baseman named Lori would return it to me.

On September 28, 1957, I stood uneasily at the desk of the editor for whom I worked and said, "Mr. Robbins, would it be all right if . . . I had tomorrow off?"

"Any special reason?" he said.

"Well, I could say my grandmother died, but the truth is it's my team that died and I'd like to go to the services."

"Yes, I guess a lot of grandmothers are being laid out at the Polo Grounds tomorrow," he said with a smile.

"The funny thing is I'm going with my grandfather, and I don't know how much worse he'd feel if my grandmother were being buried instead of the Giants. He's known them longer."

"A strange team, the Giants, but the city won't be the same without them. The last game I saw at the Polo Grounds was a no-hitter."

"Rex Barney!"

"Right."

"The damn Dodgers. My father and I saw seven innings, but then we left to beat the crowd. And we didn't have any problem 'cause the crowd was watching the no-hitter. My father does that sometimes: leaves in the seventh."

"Takes a long stretch, eh?"

"My grandfather, he's the *real* fan. He and I . . . well . . ."

"The answer is yes, you can go to the funeral. You also want a transfer to our San Francisco bureau?"

My laughter should have been tears.

At noon the following day, Gramp and I took the subway to 155th Street, walked out into Harlem, and then began the long, steep descent of the rocky slope of Coogan's Bluff. The Polo Grounds was the only park in baseball that you entered as if you were an archeologist. We were a man of eighty and a boy of twenty-four; my age was now Willie's number.

"It *would* have to be the Pirates," said Gramp in disgust. "You know what's at stake here, Ralphie? Who's the worst team in baseball."

What sad irony. Three years ago, the Giants had been the *best* team in baseball, and now they were hapless fugitives and Gramp and I were saying good-bye to the Polo Grounds. What could ever replace the Polo Grounds, a park full of memories of ninth innings that should not have been played, a park where the bullpen pitchers were in positions to field balls at the outfield walls, and the hit sign was high in a smoke ring about a mile away, and the sun slipping down behind the light towers made a hopscotch board near second base, and any place you looked you might find Willie's hat.

"Gramp, tell me something—honestly," I said. "You really think it's been better to root for the screwy Giants than the Yankees?"

The man who had seen Iron Man McGinnity pitch and win both ends of a doubleheader, who had seen a crowd standing in deep centerfield close up to block a Dodger from chasing a ball to the carriages, paused a few seconds and then said, "Ralphie, would the Yankees have given us The Schnozz or The Barber or The Old Flash? Would a Yankee manager ever belt a fan?"

"And would Yankees ever go to Mexico?" I said.

"Just to Acapulco, not to play ball. And Willie—you don't get *him* on the Yankees; nobody acts like a kid over there. And Merkle. The Yankees never lost a pennant 'cause a guy forgot to touch second."

"Yeah, the Yankees always touch all the bases. Boring. I guess we *will* have to root for San Francisco. I mean, they'll still be the up-and-down Giants."

"Sure, they'll still be fun out there," he said. "Heck, they really belong there. You know, it was in San Francisco that a fly ball hit DiMag on the head."

"It *did*? DiMaggio?"

"Yes, it was the fog."

"We bring our own fog."

"That we do."

"It's just that ... well, without the Polo Grounds, it won't be the same. No more Siberia. No more China and Japan."

And then, moments after this lament for the *National Geographic*'s home in the National League, I went inside and took my last loving looks at a place as fitting for baseball as Belmont Park: at the clubhouse steps five hundred feet away, where DiMaggio had kept running after making the final catch of the '36 Series; at the Chinese countryside, where Dusty Rhodes's tenth-inning homer had won the first game of the '54 Series; and at the plate where Carl Hubbell had struck out Ruth, Gehrig, Foxx, Simmons, and Cronin in a row in the '34 All-Star Game. At least the plate was legitimate.

It was Dusty Rhodes who drove in the one Giant run of this swan-song game of 1957, the only ball game I have ever seen that I did not in some way enjoy. To have beaten the lowly Pirates in this mournful affair would have been meaningless, of course; but losing to them had meaning indeed, especially 9–1, with Willie weakly grounding out in the ninth. It meant my team was going west with a whimper.

After the Giants had awakened enough to flee into the clubhouse, while the fans were tearing up the Polo Grounds because they could not tear up the team, I walked to the subway in silence with Gramp.

"You know, Ralphie," he finally said, "watching those guys tear up centerfield reminded me. . . . Did I ever tell you how a centerfielder named Snodgrass once cost us a World Series by dropping an easy fly?"

"Don't try to cheer me up," I replied.

4
Fear and Trembling at Second Base

◆────────────────────────◆

The Family Position Is Claimed

*F*ourteen months after I had backed into my own little China in a game of stickball, I began playing a version of stickball called baseball at a summer camp in Maine. Now twelve years old and still a total stranger to puberty, I decided I wanted to play second base on Camp Wigwam's junior varsity team, which played hardball against camps also full of frail Jewish boys who dreamed of being Pistol Pete Reiser or King Kong Keller instead of eye-ear-nose-and-throat men.

There did happen to be baseball talent in my family, but it lay far from me in my cousin Sammy Selesnick, a Bronx shortstop who had played brilliantly for James Monroe High School and then had been invited to try out for the top Yankee farm team, Kansas City. His mother, however, had hung up his spikes.

"Baseball is no career for a Jewish boy," my aunt Eva had said.

"But Hank *Greenberg* is Jewish," Sammy had told her.

"Not enough. If his father had a cleaning business like yours, Greenberg would be in something solid today. I won't have you spitting tobacco with all those *goyim*."

When I also heard these words, they confused me, for some of those *goyim* were already my friends and I had seen no tobacco fly from them; but I did not argue with Aunt Eva, for she was a warm-hearted bigot and I loved her.

And so, Sammy had gone not to the minors but the cleaners, a tragedy I thought about whenever I saw a picture of a Yankee and imagined a Yankee middle of Gordon, Selesnick, and DiMaggio. After Pearl Harbor, Sammy had gone into the navy, which was also no career for a Jewish boy; but at least Aunt Eva had the comfort of knowing that there was less spitting on the deck of his destroyer than in the on-deck circle.

Because my baseball ability was so far beneath Sammy's, the ideal position for me to play was second base in a league of pampered boys fleeing polio. And even for second in *this* league, my skill was questionable: I had a weak arm; I could not hit a hardball more than once in fifteen or twenty swings, unless it happened to be on a tee; and I felt confident fielding only infield flies.

A fear of ground balls can be a problem for a second baseman, but I felt I could hide it in this league. Most of these boys struck out most of the time; and, since few were left-handed, those who did hit to me would be swinging late, probably fooled by the pitch, and would hit softer grounders than the rare hitters who could pull. Moreover, in case the ball found its way into my glove, at second I would have time to fumble with it a bit before making my throw because I planned to play no more than twenty feet from first; I planned to play where Keith Hernandez does now. Had Keith been on that Wigwam team, I would have had to play on his shoulders.

At the end of the first week of camp, I made the team as the starting second baseman. But making that team in no way qualified as a sporting triumph, for one of my competitors was a boy who managed to swing the bat without breaking his wrists, a talent that could have kept him from ever striking out; another was a boy who ran with all the springiness of The Schnozz; and a third was able to go to his left, where the ball then went through his middle. All, like me, were Jewish. Perhaps Aunt Eva had been right: we were intended to be picking up clothes and not bouncing balls. Nevertheless, partly because I had speed, but primarily by default, I became the second baseman of the Camp Wigwam junior varsity baseball team one year before Israel's Hank Greenberg hit forty-four home runs.

In the first three games we played, I made two errors, but I also cleanly fielded one ball and held the batter to a single. Because I was an unselfish player who wanted to see my teammates shine, I hoped that every batter hit the ball to someone else. At those dismaying moments when grounders did come straight at me and I suddenly had to stop seeing the game as a spectator sport, I always dropped to my knees, as if in prayer.

The first time he saw this devout defense during our opening practice, our coach, a counselor named Davey Marks, said, "Ralph, *one* knee is enough. Nobody goes down on two."

I agreed with him, but found it hard to change: I continued to field religiously.

"Well," he said a while later, "maybe you'll do better at bat. Lots of players are good hit, no field."

At bat, however, avoidance was also the heart of my style. Because I was so short, I decided not to swing at any balls that summer but instead to work all the pitchers for walks, a strategy that Stanky was not ashamed to copy at the Polo Grounds. My grand design, therefore, was to be a second baseman who never touched the ball with his glove or his bat. In my own uniquely dreary way, I was redefining The Game.

"Ralph, I like your speed and spirit," Davey told me at practice one day, "but sooner or later you're gonna have to get involved with the ball. I know you're never very *far* from it, but . . ."

"Davey, *believe* me, I'm really trying to tear up the old pea patch," I said.

"Look, I know you're kind of . . . afraid of the ball."

"Well . . . kind of . . . in my own way." I squirmed with embarrassment, but suddenly found a way out. "You see, Ducky Medwick and I, we're both a little . . . gun-shy."

"Medwick was hit in the *head*," said Davey.

"But I know how he feels."

"And you see him coming back and digging in, don't you? Ralph, *you're* just gonna have to dig in and show some guts. Baseball is guts as well as skill. When you're out in the field, I want you to make yourself keep facing the plate. You look around too much."

"I like to check the defense."

"Just be *part* of it. And at bat, I want you to stand up and face the pitcher like a *man*."

"You know, Medwick got off easy. A guy was once *killed* at the Polo Grounds. Ray Chapman."

"Unfortunately, you'll live to keep playing."

"Davey, with my height—and the way I crouch—I'm a cinch to walk a lot; these kids are wild."

"I *know* you can walk a lot, but that's not the way to

play the game. This is the greatest game there is and I don't want you to play it like a midget with cramps. I want you to stand up and show your guts. Take a good cut at bat and attack the ball in the field. If it hits you ... well, have faith in our infirmary."

After giving me this speech in different forms about five times, Davey began to call me Guts, and so did the other boys on the team, though some of them seemed less than sincere.

"Are you Guts or Putz, I forget?" said a boy named Roger Rappaport.

My challenge in this summer of '45 was to prove myself a man to Davey, to my teammates, and also to my father, a self-made man with the punch of a heavyweight, who would be coming to see me soon. I would have to do more than stop wetting the bed, although that was the place to start, of course. I would have to use baseball for my coming of age, perhaps by taking one in the head like Medwick or by running into the catcher; but I feared taking one in the head like Ray Chapman, and you could not run into the catcher unless you were coming down from third, and reaching third was like a trip to Zanzibar for me. On July 20, in spite of mixing my strikeouts with some walks, I still had not made it. The two RBI men behind me were hitting .300: .150 apiece.

Courage might have been easier to muster in the field. Perhaps I could charge a ball slammed toward second and have it take a lucky hop and hit me in the face, for my face was not too far from the ground. I pictured myself unconscious on the infield grass, my orthodontia caked with blood and my uniform stained with grass like Sammy's and Stanky's. And I pictured myself coming to in the infirmary and looking up at my father and saying, "Did they score much while I was out?"

"No, Kiddo," my father would say, "you held 'em."

"Next time I'll use the glove."

When he was twelve, my father had gone from a diamond to an infirmary, and not in his dreams. In the summer of 1914, Paul Schoenstein was the bat boy for an all-black Harlem team called the Lincoln Giants; it was the strangest integration in the history of American sport. Early one afternoon that summer, my father was kneeling near the on-deck circle, enjoying a cigarette. Kneeling on ball fields seems to have been in the Schoenstein genes, and so was a love of Harlem Giants. In fact, the Lincoln Giants played just a few blocks south of the Polo Grounds, and my father told me that some of their players could have helped us in our wilderness years.

One of these players was now at bat and starting to swing at a fastball when my father turned to look at something in the stands and was hit in the head by a speeding foul ball. His face dropped to the dirt and he lost consciousness, the precise heroics I dreamed of at camp to distract everyone from the way I played, although losing consciousness would not have been a major change in my style. After a few seconds, my father awoke and was carried by a couple of numbers runners to nearby Harlem Hospital, where about a dozen of the Giants went to see him after the game. The sight of all those black players visiting their little white teammate, thirty-three years before Branch Rickey reversed the colors, stayed with my father all his life.

"They were wonderful players," he once told me. "Hell, we had five Jackie Robinsons on that team and a catcher as strong as Lombardi, but he wasn't paralyzed."

"Why did they have a white bat boy?" I asked him.

"I'm not sure," he said. "Maybe they got a kick out of calling me 'boy.'"

From time to time, I would wonder if my father's injury had somehow been the reason I was afraid of the ball; but then I realized that such fear could only have been caused by my pregnant mother taking one in the head, and no women played hardball when I was in the womb.

My father never showed fear, only strength. On those Saturdays or Sundays when he was able to play ball with me in the park, he used this strength to throw me towering flies, the kind no boy ever hit to the infield, except young Darryl Strawberry.

"Hang in there, Kiddo," he kept saying, advice that was good for a bleeding middleweight but lacked certain instructional detail for a ballplayer.

At Wigwam, while the rest of me hung in, my mouth was constantly in motion, another distraction from the way I played. While pounding my Ken Keltner glove at the spot where few balls ever stopped, I kept hollering at the pitcher the way I imagined that Leo the Lip and Stanky did.

"Hum babe! Hum babe!" I cried, an incantation that did not seem to carry a valuable message to our pitcher. "Chuck that apple! Toss that pill! Hum babe! Hum babe! Chuck that pill!"

Had mixed metaphors been able to inspire a pitcher, our team would never have lost; but the apples and pills—and baseballs too—were often rerouted through my position, a vacated second base with a player there.

* * *

Before the game, to be held at another summer camp forty-one years later, Lori and I worked out in our yard. I knew the best teachers of baseball were mediocre players, and I had been almost that good.

"Stop throwing sidearm," I said, "except on a bunt. You'll be wild; I've *told* you that."

"You think I have a good arm?" she said.

"Yes, you do."

"Then say so. Say 'Good arm, good arm.' "

"Okay. Good arm, good arm; big head, big head."

"How many positions do you think I could play?"

"At once?"

"Daddy . . ."

"Let's just work on second. *I* never got that one right. I kept wanting to play it with a spaldeen."

"You don't think I can make it to the majors, do you?"

"Of *course* I do."

"Then how come you always smile when I say it?"

"Well . . . because I . . ."

"Love me?"

"No, it's certainly not that. Look, too much talk, not enough practice."

"I'm gonna make it, you know."

"Honey, I know."

"So you think I *will*? You think they'll let a girl play?"

"By the time you're ready, yes."

"How come they can't play *now*?"

"You want to be a lawyer or a ballplayer?"

"Let me pitch a few, okay? When I throw it underhand, I have a disguising fastball."

"A *disguising* fastball?"

"You know: like Dwight's."

68

"You mean *rising*," I said with laughter that Lori also could not resist.

"Let's tell that one to Tim McCarver," she said.

"And let's tell him you want to train for second base by pitching. Okay, here they come: some line drives first. . . . *Two* hands—and watch the ball all the way. Never look at runners or anything else. . . . *That's* it. Good! . . . No, turn your mitt *up* for those: keep it facing up and they won't bounce out. . . . A high one now, the kind my father used to throw me."

"Was baseball the same back then?"

"Way back when I was a boy? When General Grant was commissioner? No, we played it with canoe paddles and tangerines."

"*Daddy.*"

"Yes, the same, except for Astroturf and the DH. And the splitter and batting gloves. And a million dollars for a two-fifty hitter."

"I can hit *that.*"

"Girls may have to hit three hundred."

"That stinks."

"Don't worry. No daughter of mine is allowed to hit below three hundred. . . . Okay, a pop-up from Gary."

"What *else*?"

After circling under my high fly, she caught it with a one-handed swat that made me sink with a sense of time.

"*More* of those!" she cried.

"But don't *swat* them. You're not catching flies, you're . . . catching flies. Use *two hands.*"

"*Everybody* uses one hand."

"I know, but it still makes me nervous; use two for a while."

"I'll look *goofy.*"

69

"Like DiMaggio, you mean. He seemed to need two. Look, remember the ball Dave Parker dropped that gave us the game? He catches like a guy directing traffic and I don't want that to be *you*. . . . Okay, some grounders."

"I'm really great on those now. Just watch me!"

"Keep your head down and your eye on the ball. And stay in *front* of it. You saw what happened to HoJo when he didn't do that."

"Daddy, don't you think I know *anything*? This is my *game*."

After fielding about twenty grounders thrown in different spots at different speeds, misplaying only a few, Lori took some swings at pitches with her new bat. She made contact most of the time with balls at her knees, but balls at her chest made her look like The Hondo Hurricane.

"Stop uppercutting," I told her with the wisdom of a man whose batting weakness had been anything thrown by a pitcher. "Swing straight through. You can't hit the high stuff uppercutting."

"I like 'em low," she replied.

"Fine: You'll say that on a note to the pitcher. You saw what happened to Lenny when he started uppercutting."

"And now my Mookie hits better than Lenny. Don't you think my Mookie is faster too?"

"It's very close. Lenny may have it by a shade."

"Daddy, do they really have bats made of *aluminum*?"

"Unfortunately, yes. They don't split, they gong; but splitting is better."

"Maybe that's so you can't cork them."

"A very good theory."

"Why does Whitey Herzog keep taking HoJo's bat?

Cork's not the thing. HoJo's doing better 'cause he's playing all the time this year. Doesn't Whitey *know* that?"

A boy in Lori's school had not known that and she had been drawn into an argument with him, finally telling him that he was a major jerk for not realizing the reason for HoJo's higher average this year. Lori had been starting to measure the intellects of people by how much baseball they knew, a standard that turned her mother into one of the learning disabled.

"Okay now," I said, "keep your eye on the ball and swing straight through."

Moments later, she belted a drive to right centerfield that filled me with pleasure.

"Triple!" she cried.

"Double. Ott's out there."

"You think I'll hit one like that today?"

"You'll do fine today. Just relax and concentrate."

"You can't do *both*."

"Okay, pick one," I said, smiling at my locker-room triteness. "But don't do the Teufel Shuffle. Those kids won't understand. They don't know baseball the way you do."

"You think anyone does?"

"No, Howard, nobody."

About an hour later, I was in the stands at Lori's day camp for her first competitive game of softball. Watching her take batting practice, her bat straight up like Musial's and Morey's, her behind protruding unlike Musial's and Morey's, I wished that my father and grandfather had been sitting beside me. My grandfather would have wanted to teach her how to pull the ball down the line; and my father would have been making plans to beat the crowd.

71

In Lori's first at bat of the game, she revealed the effectiveness of my teaching by doing the Teufel Shuffle with her little hips, which had major-league motion. She was, in fact, better than Teufel, who was the right sex for driving the ball, but the wrong one for driving his hips like a scrappy Gypsy Rose Lee.

"Is your daughter Hawaiian?" a woman next to me said.

"No, she just loves the Mets," I replied as Lori hit a line drive past the shortstop and dashed directly to second, undoubtedly thinking of Mookie all the way.

Unfortunately, the second baseman then told Lori that she had "looked like a dorkhead" doing the Shuffle, an observation that Lori took personally: she was at the brink of tears when she told me the story between innings.

"Forget her; she's stupid," I said, while Lori fought to keep her eyes dry. "What a great *hit* you got!"

"She belongs on the Cardinals," said Lori. "If she calls me a dorkhead again, I'm going to punch her."

"If you want to punch, switch to hockey. Look, you're going to be the female Jackie Robinson, right?"

"Right."

"You know what they called Jackie when he first came up?"

"What?"

"You're not old enough to hear it. Now just keep swinging level and *meet* the ball. Don't try to kill it like the other kids."

"Thanks, Dad. I love you."

"Don't let anyone hear you saying *that* to your coach."

In the fourth inning, Lori made contact again and hit a grounder to the pitcher, who ran to the line and tagged her out, showing a faith in the first baseman that the old Mets had in Marvelous Marv. Meanwhile, in the field, Lori had one chance, a pop-up that she caught with two hands, after which she smiled at me.

Tragedy did not strike until the final inning. With the score tied and one out, Lori stood near second base, pounding her George Brett mitt not far from the girl who represented the winning run. She had asked me a few days before it if was against the rules to play second with a third baseman's glove.

"Couldn't the umpire take the glove the way they take HoJo's bat?" she had said.

"And look for cork?" I had said.

"No, I mean, isn't a third baseman's glove just ... well, like for bunts and balls down the line?"

"No, honey, it's fine. I used a glove named for Ken Keltner, the third baseman who stopped DiMaggio's streak. Of course, it didn't stop much for me, but you're a much better fielder."

From time to time now, Lori glanced to her right at the girl on second, and on second she was: standing on the bag. I knew that Lori was tempted to sneak in behind her the way Teufel did, but Teufel had no runners who climbed the bag.

"Home babe! Home babe!" Lori called to the pitcher, almost remembering the Wigwam chant I had told her about.

But the pitcher needed more than a mangled cliché, for the batter drove her delivery into short left field. The girl on second, however, moved only to third, where again she climbed the base. She seemed to like to take one base at a time and then settle down.

With the winning run on third, Lori now moved in a

few steps for a play at the plate. Meanwhile, the third baseman moved back, either because she knew less baseball than Lori or because she wanted to guard against a bloop double.

The suspense did not last long: The new batter hit the first pitch at Lori, who charged it and would have thrown to the plate had the ball not gone into right field.

After the game, as she sat glumly on the grass, I said, "You just have to forget it, honey. *Everyone* makes errors."

"But it was the *winning run*," she said.

"You mean like the winning run on Teufel's error in the Series?"

Her lower lip retracted a bit and she turned thoughtful. "I looked like him, didn't I?"

"If you can shuffle like him, you can field like him too," I said. "And he didn't charge it."

"I shouldn't've charged it either."

"No, you were *right* to charge it. I used to *wait* for a slow one—I waited minutes sometimes—and if it didn't go through me, the only play I had was a throw back to the pitcher. I was *afraid* and you're *not*. They called me Guts, but it was like calling Fred Flintstone 'Professor.' "

"You're just saying that."

"You mean instead of *singing* it? Of *course* I'm saying it. Because it's true."

"I would've had it at third. That's what the mitt is for. It doesn't work right at second."

"Okay, for the car and the trip to Bermuda, who was the Met who said, 'The first-rate player hopes that the next ball is hit to him'?"

"No, it was, 'Whenever I make an error, I hope the next ball is hit to me,' and it was Santana."

"Right; I almost knew it. It was *Ra-fa-yell*."

She smiled at the memory of the chant for Santana that she had tried to start at Shea like the one for Mookie, but it had not caught on. It was a chant that belonged in a seventh inning in San Juan.

"Well, *you're* like that," I said, "and I never was. After an error, I never hoped the next one was hit to me. I didn't want two errors in a row. I'd made the error because the *last* one had been hit to me."

She smiled again. "Let's work on grounders tonight."

"In the yard or the living room?"

As the starting second baseman of Wigwam's junior varsity baseball team, I had been in six games by the end of the third week of July, blending strikeouts, taps to the pitcher, and walks. It turned out, however, that the walk was not my only weapon, for I also was hit three times by pitches. These blows were not brushbacks, of course. No pitcher had to back off a hitter who was backing off nicely on his own.

The third time I was hit, after the ball had struck that fine line known as my chest, I savored the soreness for many minutes; and when the inning was over, I ran to Davey and said, "How's *that* for getting a hit!"

"Listen, Guts," he said, "you may be built like a bat, but you still gotta start hitting the ball with something else."

"But *Stanky* walks and gets hit a lot."

"Can't you aim any higher than Stanky?"

"No."

That evening, I sat amid the comic books and pretzels on my bed and wrote:

Dear Mom and Dad:

I'm really doing great at camp this year. I've played in six JV games!

Dad, you'd really be proud of me because everybody calls me Guts now. That's because I kind of stank at baseball in the beginning but I made myself get better like crazy. I'm not as good as Sammy yet but who is except Rizzutto? (Rizutto? Rizzuto? Pick one.)

There's a big father-son game on Parents Weekend and I can't wait for it! You'll get a chance to see me play and you can play too Dad! So start warming up!

Tell Rabbit Maranville I'm learning how to pivot on the double play and I hope to make one before the summer is over.

Love,
Your Guts

A few days later, I received a large envelope from the *New York Journal-American,* where my father was city editor and employed Rabbit Maranville, a Hall of Fame shortstop, as a sports columnist. The envelope contained a dramatic charcoal drawing by an artist named Burris Jenkins, Jr., who had put two heads side-by-side: one was Douglas MacArthur, in his general's cap, looking like someone approving of The Creation; and the other was Ralph Schoenstein, in his baseball cap, looking like an ad for the Fresh Air Fund. Beneath the faces were the following lines:

MAC AND GUTS
They Bounced Back

My father's faith in my being a five-star general of summer-camp baseball was as touching as it was misplaced. It was based entirely on love, unlike my loving but also logical faith in the natural athlete who is Lori. On Lori's bedroom wall are gold and silver medals from the Junior Olympics. On *my* boyhood bedroom wall was a picture of Mel Ott and a NO SPITTING sign.

At two o'clock on the afternoon of August 1, the fathers and sons began their warm-up on Wigwam's ball field for the annual game. Taking his practice at second, the family position, my father was swiping at ground balls as if he were bailing out a boat. It was, of course, hard for him to see any small object coming his way because of the smoke from the cigarette in his lips.

"Your old man thinks he's Humphrey Bogart?" Roger Rappaport said to me.

"It just so happens, if you want to know, that my father played for the Lincoln Giants," I angrily and fallaciously replied.

"And he smoked in the field? What the hell were they, a prison team?"

"It just so happens, if you want to know," I said once again, liking the ring of this substitute for thought, "that smoking relaxes him. *DiMaggio* smokes."

"I think it's *after* the game."

"Get lost, Roger, okay?"

"If you're Guts, is the old man Butts?" And he laughed.

"Up yours with gauze," I said, showing how nicely the language of stickball transferred to the baseball field.

When Roger walked away, however, I ran out to my father and said, "Hey Dad, *please* don't clown around. This is a *serious game.* That cigarette . . ."

77

"Are you kidding, Kiddo?" he said, smiling through the smoke. "You just take care of *yourself* and be ready to handle what I hit you."

I knew that my father *could* hit a ball four hundred feet, but only when he was playing tennis. On occasional Sunday mornings when we had played tennis on Riverside Drive, he had managed to put his awesome strength into at least one shot and send it toward the Hudson as a three-sewer forehand.

In no way reassured by my father's words, I ran back to the sons' side of the field and continued to spit in my glove. A ball would arrive there with a splash; but spitting, which Lori feels is a worthwhile part of major-league style, was also part of the style that supported the name of Guts. I could, of course, have kept my cocky saliva to myself had I played well enough to live my fantasy of lining sharp singles to centerfield; but in those accidental moments when my bat intercepted the ball, my hands were left stinging from the feeble groundout; and so, I had to let my mouth be the most aggressive part of me. In addition to turning my glove into a leather cuspidor, I was also the voice of the infield with my constant and idiotic "Hum babe!"

An even better cheerleader was Davey, who now stood before the team and said, "I want you guys to go out there and show your old men what you're made of. Don't be soft on 'em just because they're paying the bills. I want you to give me a hundred and ten percent. And that extra ten percent . . ." He patted his stomach, a beach ball beneath a Rutgers T-shirt. "That comes from here." And then he turned to me. "Okay, Guts, let's start it off! Make some contact up there!"

Suddenly, my mouth went dry; someone else would

have to water my glove. But when I reached the plate to be the campers' leadoff man, I switched to another show of style and vigorously rubbed dirt into my hands, thus giving myself a better grip for striking out.

As I took my place in the batter's box, I looked out at my father, who was smiling at me from second base, and I was sure he wanted to say, *Do you need anything, Kiddo? Would you like an intentional walk?*

What I was feeling now was more complex than the feeling of a basketball player bent on shaving points. I wanted to play well and courageously for a team that won, while my father played well and smokelessly for one that lost.

In spite of what Davey had told me about batting being a contact sport, I instinctively sank into my crouch, eliminated my strike zone, and drew a walk. When I reached first base, my father smiled at me again and suggested that I come to second with a sweep of his arm, as if calling a cab. I responded with a look that Ty Cobb might have made before trying to shred a short-stop's legs. If the next batter, Fats Mandlebaum, moved me to second base, I knew that my father might give me a hug or slip a fiver into my uniform.

"Look alive, Guts!" cried Davey. "No double play! Go in there hard!"

"Let's see ya put your father on his ass!" cried Roger Rappaport.

I was pondering this paternal inversion when Fats hit a grounder back to the CPA who was pitching. As I took off for second with the only admirable part of my body, my legs, the CPA spun around and threw neatly to my father, who waved the shortstop off the toss for a force out by colliding with him at the bag. Having touched the bag for the force on me, my father now had an easy chance to throw to first to double Fats, who was going down the line as if getting there were half the fun. My father, however, decided that this was the time for a family reunion: he waited for me to reach the base and then applied a meaningless and maddening tag. At least it was not a hug play.

"*Jesus*, Pop," I said as we met, "it's not a *tag* play. You made the *force*."

"Double play," he said with a laugh.

"Oh, God, I can't go back to the bench."

"Relax; it's just a game."

"Not the way *you* play it."

"Okay, that's enough," he said, losing the smile. "I *told* you, it's just a game. It's not a religion."

For the next ninety minutes, it *was* just a game, often resembling baseball; and I played it under even more pressure than Lori or Leo ever felt, for I was attempting a feat unknown in baseball history: to circle the bases without passing the second baseman. It was, therefore, my good fortune to strike out my next three times at bat, perhaps intentionally.

And yet, how I loved this game! I could not have loved it more if I had known how to play it. Years later, talking about the army in *From Here to Eternity*, Prewitt would say, "You can love a thing without the thing loving you back." Nevertheless, as I kept trying to hit the ball and pick it up, I never stopped hoping that this wondrous thing on the diamond would start to love me back.

The boys beat their fathers on that ancient summer day, and I won something else of my own. Without knowing it, I was beginning to learn how to be a baseball father who would give Lori more wisdom than squirm time. And, in spite of what my own father had said, I was beginning to learn that baseball *could* be a kind of sustaining faith, a kind of raucous religion, no matter how unorthodox you were.

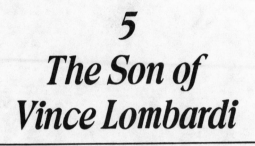

5
*The Son of
Vince Lombardi*

*Tossing Daughters
into the Fray*

*I*f Lori does become the first female in the major leagues, if someday her ponytail flies loose at Shea while she is dumped on a double play, her grand achievement will have been caused partly by her passion for baseball, partly by her talent for playing it, and partly by a gene from her father that belongs in a loyal East German. Lori's father, as fiercely competitive as athletes who have sporting skill as well, was the boy who in stickball had played both shallow Broadway and deep laundry, the boy who at camp had conquered a fear of the ball and then looked for pitches he could hit with his chest.

My competitive zeal, in fact, has gone far beyond the playing fields of Manhattan and Maine: it has added a certain nitwit combativeness to parts of life where sounder minds never keep score. How often my wife has wished that I were Ernie Lombardi instead of Vince, most fervently when I am chasing Lori through the house in a maniacal effort to cry, "Got you last!"

"There's something about that game that disproves evolution," Judy told me one night as I dove for Lori and almost caught her before falling to the kitchen floor.

"I think the last fathers to play 'got you last' with their children lived in New Guinea a long time ago."

Not content to restrict our competition just to sport, Lori and I have even competed at the piano, where we have brought a sense of sport by shoving each other back and forth on the bench while each of us tries to be the first to learn a new composition.

"Bet I know the 'Minuet in G' before *you*!" said Lori one day in a soulful mood.

"Bet I can play it first in E *flat*!" I replied.

"That doesn't *count*. You play *everything* in E flat."

One winter afternoon, ignited by the Napoleonic fire of a new Beethoven piece, Lori actually shoved me off the bench, where I had been sitting like Lee Mazzilli. As I lay beneath her on the floor, hearing her boldly play the piece, I knew the secret admiration that had been felt for Joe Louis by the fallen Billy Conn.

My endless private Olympics began long before I first got Lori last: They began on the day in 1960 that my daughter Jill was born. Standing entranced at the window of the hospital nursery, I had been noticing that Jill had remarkably long eyelashes for a newborn child. They were not only elegant but clearly an edge in the competition.

"Those lashes on my daughter look like fans for Cleopatra, don't you think?" I said to a mother beside me, who was erroneously admiring her own child.

This observation put her off-balance, for she had done no lash measuring of her own with which to fight back. Desperately, she retreated into bones.

"My baby has fingers you just wouldn't *believe*," she said.

"More than ten?" I coolly replied.

Because eyelash flaunting was not a recognized AAU event, I had to wait until Jill was ten before moving to a battlefield worthy of my lunatic lust to be number one: the 1970 Junior Olympics in my hometown of Princeton, New Jersey. Possessing a considerably more attractive model of my own legs, Jill had seemed to me to be faster than all the other girls her age. However, the fact that I had not seen all the other girls her age was a prominent flaw in my game plan; and another was that the sum of my knowledge of coaching track was "On your mark, get set, go." There was probably more to it than that, but Jill's natural speed would no doubt make up for the stark simplicity of my coaching style.

"Just have fun today, sweetie," I told her when we arrived at the high school track, where dozens of children were warming up, all of whom I hated in the spirit of friendly sport.

"Mom told you to say that," she said. "You really want me to win."

"Well, if you have a choice . . . yes; but the point is mostly to enjoy the event."

After speaking that line, I silently apologized to the Blue Fairy.

"Daddy, the girls in my group are all *bigger*. I'm so *small*."

"Now, don't talk like that. You're going to grow."

"But not today."

As Jill registered for the hundred-yard dash for ten- and eleven-year-olds, my mind desperately sought words of inspiration from movies, monuments, and cereals; but I could remember nothing that Churchill, Rockne, or Davey Johnson had ever said that applied to a frightened child who should have been romping with her friends instead of dashing to live her father's foolish fantasies. And while I wondered if I should tell Jill, *Win this one for God, country, and Mercer County*, I also wondered if a defeat would give her a psychic scar.

My father thought I was Wilma Rudolph, she would tell the Mother Superior.

My musing ended when Jill took her place beside five other girls for an elimination heat.

"Just keep your eye on the finish line," I told her, "and give it all you've got."

Judy, of course, would have told her, "Just enjoy the trip."

Seconds later, the starter's gun sounded; and seconds after that, I was wishing it had put a bullet in me, for Jill was running to a different drummer, one playing a march. She had no competition for finishing sixth.

"You did fine, honey," I told her as we walked off the field. "I'm proud of you."

"Why?" she said. "They all beat me."

"Well, in a *way*, yes, but . . . you are a winner just by *doing* it. Those girls were all bigger. And they had another advantage too: they're faster than you."

"Daddy, do I have to do this again?"

"No, and I'm sorry I put you through it this time. Hey, *I* know what: let's start playing *baseball*. That's really the greatest game there is—and you can be *any* size!"

"I don't like baseball," said Jill. "I like lacrosse."

What a blow for a Giant fan! To discover that his firstborn not only disliked baseball but liked lacrosse, a sensible sport if her father had been an Iroquois and could have taken her out to the old stick game.

My second child, four years younger than Jill, was

also a girl, Eve-Lynn. Though her lashes were standard, she was equally beautiful, with high cheekbones, happy eyes, and a cherub's smile; and she was equally useless for sharing my memories of boyhood days at the Polo Grounds or for creating new ones at Shea Stadium. By the time she was ten, Eve-Lynn had drifted far from the diamond, leaving me in sporting loneliness. You cannot buy me some peanuts and Cracker Jack at the old soccer field, where she often went to spend subversive afternoons.

"Baseball is boring," she told me, speaking the equivalent of a belch in St. Patrick's Cathedral.

And then came Lori, just two weeks after the bicentennial of the Declaration of Independence. More significantly, just two hours after the Mets had won a doubleheader in Cincinnati.

As Lori approached school age, I pondered the character flaw in my wife that had given me children who thought a double play was two one-acters; and I waited with heavy heart for Lori to turn to bullfighting and start looking for the Tijuana scores.

"You know," I told Judy one night as she read Flaubert and I Dick Young, "if Lori doesn't take to baseball, it might be fun to try it again and have another one."

"Just check the Yellow Pages for Surrogates," she sweetly replied.

My recruitment of potential ball fans from Judy's farm system was over. My last candidate was this third girl, another one with a face fit for framing.

And so, when Lori was six, I began to teach her how to catch and hit a Wiffle ball. I was delighted to find that she had grace, good reflexes, and speed. Because she had a father who could teach her such fine points as how to

89

uncross her hands on the bat, she was able to hit a pitched ball with regularity by the time she was seven. She was three years behind Mantle, but ahead of several million girls.

In that seventh year, Judy put her into a gymnastics class at the YWCA, but I considered the class merely marking time before Lori abandoned herself to baseball.

"This stuff is good to know for brushback pitches and double plays," I told Judy one day as we watched Lori tumbling across the Y's mats. "But the problem with gymnastics is she can't go all the way with it; she can't win the Olympics. The Romanian girls take steroids and the German girls are men."

"I wonder," said Judy, "if Freud had a word for a man who turns everything into a life-and-death struggle. Jackass, I suspect. And by the way, Superman, I wouldn't mind if you stopped that hurdling you've been doing over Lori's head. The first time you kick her in the face, I'm going to take a good hard look at this marriage."

For some reason, Judy was disturbed because lately my competitive lust had been driving me to flaunt my creaky litheness by hurdling Lori's head, the newest display of a splendidly demented desire to go airborne over loved ones that had begun when I was Lori's gymnastics age. One day a few weeks before Pearl Harbor, I had been running through my home when I came upon my sister lying before me on the rug. Although I had always enjoyed stepping on my sister, this time I was suddenly seized by the urge to jump over her.

From that day on, I was driven to keep jumping over things, not just small girls but also the furniture I scattered about my own private track; and outdoors, the bushes and hydrants and trash cans already were nicely scattered for me. There was a rhythm to my hurdling that was rare in the event: I took three or four strides and then a couple of stutter steps, a blend of hurdling and the Mexican hat dance. I never knew how far apart the hurdles—or my feet—were supposed to be, and so I ran with a syncopation that belonged not in the Millrose Games but in Looney Tunes.

Nevertheless, I kept studying the Millrose Games and also the other track meets that were held every winter in Madison Square Garden; and there I idolized Harrison Dillard, the greatest hurdler in the world. Watching Dillard sail commandingly over the sixty-yard high hurdles, I knew that here was a man who would have been able to clear not only my mother's dining-room chairs but my vertical sister too.

Dillard was the inspiration my own hurdling had needed. Now as I ran around Manhattan jumping over sundry things, I was not a little kid with a large screw loose but a sleekly muscled champion who could fly. A harbinger of the tone that the city would have in years to come, I was continuously high.

"Can't you find some other sport, Kiddo?" my father said to me one day after I had cleared the piano bench in a warm-up for the kitchen stool. "Something that's all on the ground? All that jumping around, you could run into trouble."

How prophetic were his words, for on the following Saturday morning, my future as a hurdler, dim as it already seemed, almost disappeared. At ten o'clock on that memorable day in American sport, I left a bakery with a bag of cream puffs and began to cross Broadway, which was divided by islands of grass that had fences of three iron bars. Instead of continuing through the crosswalk from the bakery to my block, I suddenly cut right and tried to hurdle the fence.

I did not miss it by much, a yard at the most. I would have had a more pleasant descent by falling forward into the grass, where the Broadway trolley did not run. Instead, however, I fell backward; and after landing, I had a chance to reflect on a fundamental principle of this sport: A man who tries to hurdle an attached iron bar may find his leg as unhinged as his mind.

As I lay there on the trolley track with a throbbing back and a sleeve full of cream, I thought about my detour from glory, for I doubted that Harrison Dillard had ever gone hurdling with a bag of cream puffs, or even a single prune Danish. Moreover, I thought about whether I would be able to arise before a trolley subdivided me.

It was at this moment that I switched to baseball. Harrison Dillard was about to be replaced by Mel Ott, who raised his leg just a safe few inches before he did his stuff.

When she was ten years old and fully embracing baseball, Lori also had to get one defective sport out of her system. It was competitive swimming, which left her system like a Roman candle on the day that we went to Princeton's public pool for a father-daughter relay race. My competitive demon could not resist leading us into an aquatic test against other fathers and daughters because I knew that we both had speed on land. I ignored the fact that Lori's best performances in water were swimming through my legs, and my best performances were keeping them open.

"Okay, honey," I said as Lori stood at the edge of the pool and prepared to swim the first two laps against four other girls. "Just bring me a ten-yard lead and we'll win."

"Daddy, why don't *you* go first?" she said.

"I'd be happy to, but it wouldn't be fair to me to swim against these girls. You'll do fine, I'm sure. You're really looking good and there's nothing to worry about."

I was developing a style in these pep talks that belonged in a political campaign and not at poolside with a child who wanted to be doing her diving into second base. Lori's nervousness made sense, of course, because once again all the girls in the contest were bigger than the Schoenstein entry. Their fathers were not bigger than I was, but all were younger. Intergenerational competition, however, was nothing new for a man whose body and mind were three decades apart.

We swam valiantly that afternoon, but Lori and I had no more chance against those other teams than The Hondo Hurricane had against Warren Spahn. After swimming her laps, she brought me a ten-yard lag and I built it effortlessly into twenty.

When the race was over, I felt not just disappointment but dismay, and I was angry at myself, for this was the second time I had set up one of my treasures for such a blow. Why had I done it? Was it because I had been the boy who was afraid of ground balls and was a one-sewer man and had creamed the Broadway trolley tracks? Last place in the Junior Olympics for Jill and now last place in a swimming meet for Lori. What sporting delight did I have in store for Eve-Lynn? Running with the bulls at Pamplona?

It had better be baseball from now on, I thought, a game in which you are bonded to eight others on your team and can blame almost every one of them for a defeat.

"It's not the score that counts," I told Lori as we dried off. "It's how you play the game."

"And we played rotten," she said.

"That may be true; but we can come back next summer, when you're a faster swimmer and all the other fathers are a year older."

She smiled, seeming to know that next summer I would still be just the same age.

Later that day, while I helped her practice grounders with a hardball on blessed dry land, Lori suddenly said, "Dad, how old will you be when I'm ninety?"

"A hundred and thirty-three," I replied with a chill.

"Will we still be able to play baseball?"

"Well, I'll probably have to DH. You lose a few steps in the field after ninety-five."

"But that means you'll be playing *American League*."

"Honey, *all* players over ninety have to play American League. . . . Keep your glove *down* on those. Keep it touching the *ground* or the ball will go through. You see how Santana does it."

"Ra-fa-*yell*!"

"I still say it won't catch on like *Mooo*-kie."

"Daddy, who invented baseball?"

"Alexander Cartwright."

"Is his birthday a holiday?"

"Not yet. Too many football fans."

"Maybe I should start staying home from school on his birthday."

"Yes, and you can study why a ball curves."

"Why *does* it?"

"Something about the spin, but I can't really explain it; I was an English major. Let's see if we can find out."

When we had finished playing and were walking back to the house to see the Mets, Lori said, "My friends' fathers don't play with them like you do."

"They probably have jobs," I said. "Many fathers do. And it's 'play with them *as* you do,' not *like*."

"Do I have to learn English *and* baseball?"

"Santana did."

"Daddy . . . please never be a real grown-up. Okay?"

"It's too late for me now. I still don't understand what a debenture is."

"But you don't just read the sports, you read the *news*."

"I'm definitely going to stop," I said. "The news these days is even worse than being swept by the Cardinals."

Lori need not have worried about my belatedly leaving adolescence, for in my fifties I walk down the street still not pondering the balance of trade but softly singing songs of my camps, my colleges, and my Giants that have never stopped sounding in my misty mind. In fact, one day on a checkout line at an A&P, I suddenly found myself singing:

> *"Cheer for your fav'rites*
> *Out at Coogan's Bluff.*
> *You'll see those Polo Grounders*
> *Do their stuff."*

And the clerk looked at me as if to say, *That's a condition on which a lot of research still needs to be done*, but she was simply hearing the voice of one of Lori's peers.

"I wonder if there's another man your age in America

who gets only toys for his birthday," said Judy last May as I unwrapped my new wooden bat that said RALPHIE SCHOENSTEIN.

Lori had been worried about losing me to a world in which men thought more about the fall of the dollar than the drop of the spaldeen; but she should have known that no legitimate grown-up would ever compete with his daughter in a bedtime version of baseball in which hits were made by landing kisses on the other team's defended face.

We invented this head-to-head competition one night when Lori was ten, just after I had carried her from a televised game to bed.

"But it's only the *seventh inning*," she said. "And we could blow the *lead*."

"Game called on account of growing," I told her.

"Just *one* more inning."

"You'll read about it at breakfast. Otherwise I'll have to give you a note: *Dear Mrs. Levin, Please excuse Lori for falling asleep in class. You shouldn't schedule school during the season.*"

Once she was in bed and I was tucking her in, she suddenly said, "Bet you can't *kiss* me!" And she crossed her arms in front of her face.

Unable to resist any challenge but maturity, I said, "Are you *kidding*?" and quickly moved my lips to the right of one of her palms to catch her on the upper left cheek.

"Base hit!" I cried.

"I want to check your mouth for cork," she said.

"Forget it, Whitey. Your mother has never been able to put a cork in there."

"Okay, man on first, no out; we'll get two."

"Not with Kevin Mitchell up. Watch me kiss your shutout good-bye."

"He can't hit Dwight."

"*Anyone* can; it's a day game."

"It's ten *o'clock*."

"We're in San Francisco."

"It would *still* be night."

"Okay, we're in *Guam* . . . Mitchell steps up now. . . . He digs into the blanket . . ."

Again I attacked and this time I scored on her forehead.

"Foul ball!" she cried.

"Your *brain* is *foul*? With *your* IQ? Almost eighty?"

"Okay, bloop single. First and second. Now I've got you where I want you: all set up for a triple play."

She tightened her defense by stiffening her crossed arms.

"Hubie Brooks doesn't hit into triple plays."

"Hubie *Brooks*? Since when was he traded to the Giants?"

"A few minutes ago. He said it's too cold in Montreal and he wants to play in a little warm fog. . . . Okay, Hubie digs in . . . and he's first-ball hitting!"

This time, however, her defense held and I could land only on her hand.

"Triple play!" she cried.

"Nonsense. You couldn't triple Hubie unless he fainted."

"He's tired from that long trip to Guam."

"Go to sleep now; it's late. Another game tomorrow."

For a few seconds, she was silent; and then she said, "Daddy, how do you keep sad thoughts away? I get them sometimes at night."

"Everyone does," I said, thinking my own variety about how quickly Lori was growing up and how quickly all these wondrous moments with her were flying by. She now was almost too heavy to carry from Tim McCarver to bed. "Just try to think about happy things."

"Sometimes I try to think about nothing, but it's very hard. How do you make your head empty?"

"Some grown-ups do it all the time, but you're too smart."

"You see, I'm a what-if person. And at night, I'm a what-if scary things. So tell me, what should I think about?"

"How about your favorite things? Like playing baseball and playing with kittens and making snowballs with your pretty red mittens."

"You got that from *The Sound of Music*!"

"Sorry; I'm a sucker for Rodgers and Hammerstein."

"Borr-ing, Daddy, borr-*ring*. My *Monkees* would never sing a song so boring. That one is worse than my sad thoughts. And it can't keep me from thinking about if you and Mommy ever . . . well, if you ever . . . *you* know."

"I get sad thoughts *too*, you know."

"What kind?"

"Well, tonight I'm thinking about some bad men calling me down to the Internal Revenue Service."

"What's that?"

"A place with lots of monsters."

"I've never heard of it."

"Too scary for children to know about. The point is, honey, you've just got to jam that dopey head with all the happy thoughts you can. Think about our being in first place by three games . . . and how you've learned to hit higher pitches . . . and how much fun we had on

Sunday riding our bikes down to the lake . . . and also how nicely you've learned to play the Bach minuet. You know, when I was a little boy and I worried too much about things, my grandmother used to say that she was going to take all my worries and send them to a lady in Hoboken who did worrying for other people. She was a professional worrier."

"Daddy, no offense, but that's really dumb."

"You're right; it is. There was no lady like that in Hoboken. She lived in Fort Lauderdale."

Lori laughed. "Making me laugh doesn't count. The sad thoughts are still there."

"Let's just stop talking and sing. 'Take me out to the ball game, take me out to the crowd . . .' "

" 'Buy me some peanuts and Cracker Jack,' " she sang. " 'I don't care if I never get back.' "

We finished our sacred song together, and then she said, "That's the song of the freshest team in the world!"

I was certainly not going to tell her that "Take Me Out to the Ball Game" belonged to every fan, even the disadvantaged in St. Louis, while the freshest team in the world had "Meet the Mets," a song that contained nearly as much musical style as "Rag Mop."

"Daddy, wasn't that nice the way they gave Jeffries his first RBI ball? He's a sweetie pie."

"So are you."

"And what a *jerk* that Lucchesi is yelling at that poor catcher."

"You mean Berryhill."

"He's *another* sweetie pie."

"I think you're going to marry a ballplayer."

"No, *I'm* the ballplayer they'll marry."

"Of course."

"Hey, let's make up one of our goofy songs."

"You think *sleep* is goofy."

"Just *one.*"

"You always manage to take bedtime to extra innings. Okay, let's see ..." And I sang:

> *"Now run along home*
> *And jump into bed.*
> *Close your eyes*
> *And ... unscrew your head."*

Lori laughed; and then, her competitive fire burning even while she was sleepy, she sang:

> *"The very same thing*
> *I say unto you.*
> *You dream of me*
> *And I'll dream of ... glue!"*

"Good one. Krazy Glue, of course."

"Wanna run in and see *Kiner's Korner?*"

"No, you're my prisoner here. Now go—"

"Sing one more. They're so fun."

"So *much* fun. Only shortstops speak like that. Okay, this is positively *it:*

> *"Take me out to the mall game,*
> *Take me out to the crowd.*
> *I don't want peanuts or Cracker Jack,*
> *I'm going to Sears to take this vacuum back."*

"Daddy, do you think we should trade Darryl for missing that game to make a rap record?"

"When you hit like Darryl," I said, "you can sing 'Melancholy Baby' at the plate. Now go to *sleep* or I'll start rooting for the Cardinals."

She smiled and kissed me—a double in the gap—and then she turned over. Within seconds she was asleep, while I sat transfixed on her bed, watching her breathe and unable to stop thinking about children being killed by earthquakes and terrorists and drunks. I was thinking about the unthinkable, so I took the advice I had given to Lori, advice that had come to me from Shoeless Joe in *Damn Yankees*: I thought about The Game.

I went to hide there once again by running a mental montage of the plays that I had loved most. Lori had often asked me what was the greatest moment in baseball.

"There are so many," I had said, "and the wonderful thing is they all last forever."

And now I fled into a few. I saw the two greatest catches of my lifetime: Willie running toward the clubhouse to take the Series blast from Wertz, and Lori standing in quiet terror to take an inflated ball from Henry Wang.

I saw Thomson's drive landing in Japan for a pennant and Lavagetto's drive landing on the wall to end a Series no-hitter and McCovey's drive landing in the maddeningly lucky glove of Richardson to steal a series from the Giants.

I saw Swoboda's racing dive in right centerfield during the Mets' first miracle and I saw an immortal Princeton schoolboy diving for home after running from first and I saw Amoros diving for Berra's hooking drive and giving Brooklyn its first Series victory because his glove was on the wrong hand.

I saw DiMaggio's titanic blast caught by Gionfriddo half in the bullpen and I saw Freddie's titanic blast almost caught by a Broadway trolley conductor and I saw Lori's titanic double through a third-grade infield.

And, in the baseball version of turning water into wine, I saw Ernie Lombardi beat out a bunt.

One afternoon a few weeks later, I descended from the heights of baseball and allowed myself to be briefly involved in a game called field hockey, which I had always vaguely thought was played by British librarians. Lori had joined the field-hockey team of the John Witherspoon Middle School because baseball was over and I had refused to let her transfer to a school in Santo Domingo. Field hockey was her answer to the question she had asked me about what she would do at that awful time when the baseball season was over; but it was an answer that did not delight me. As I watched Lori and twenty-one other girls endlessly moving a ball unsatisfactory distances with sticks, I felt a new appreciation for the greatness of The Game.

Because John Witherspoon was playing this first game against a school called Notre Dame, I hoped that the daughters of Rockne would somehow rise above this earthbound endeavor and challenge Lori's competitive spirit. However, when the game began, I saw that field hockey would always have the sporting drama of walking a dog and even a female Gipper could not transcend. There was a structured and tedious tone to the play: no end-to-end flow as in ice hockey, no forward dashing the length of the field to attack the net, not even a good elbow in the ribs. Instead, a girl in one small cluster would smack the ball a few yards in the general direction of other life, where a new girl would toy with it awhile and then send it along, sometimes to a team-mate. From time to time, the referee stopped the game because a girl had hit the ball on the backhand side of her stick, a rule designed to maintain the stately quality of play.

All the time that this leisurely action was going on, Lori was standing alone at the end of the field near her own net, undoubtedly wondering if a man who hits a game-winning home run has to touch all the bases. Suddenly, the ball rolled up to her and she stopped it and began to take it the other way. For some reason, possibly because they were seizing this quiet time to say their prayers, most of the Notre Dame girls were standing meditatively on the other side of the field, so Lori had a lane for a breakaway to the goal.

"*Go*, Lori!" I cried. "Take it all the *way*!"

"Oh, she can't do that," said a woman beside me. "She has to stay in her zone."

I have known outfielders who felt they had to stay in their zone, but Lori never played that way: merry abandon was her style. And now she was moving the ball like Gretzky, while I cried, "*Go*, baby! *Score*!"

She had run halfway to the enemy net when the referee's whistle blew.

"She can't move that far from her spot," said the color commentator beside me. "There are lots of special rules in this game."

"I don't want to hear them," I said. "The game belongs in a nursing home in Pakistan."

For the next forty minutes, I lived Lori's frustration as I watched her imprisonment in this questionable sport; and while I watched, I tried to figure out the number of days until spring training. When the game was over and

Notre Dame had gently beaten John Witherspoon 2–0, Lori and I met on the sideline.

"Nice game anyway, honey," I said, hoping she would think I was meaning this one.

"I didn't *do* anything," she replied. "*Nobody* did."

"I think that's the way it's supposed to be played. At least it's a little exercise. And don't forget: just a hundred and sixty days till spring training."

"Let's make a special calendar for them!"

"Great idea!"

"I'm really worried about something."

"What?"

"You think we'll trade Mookie this winter?"

"I'm afraid we might. Lenny is much younger."

She curled her lip. "That's not *Mookie's* fault."

"No, definitely his mother's."

"He's a prettier *runner* than Lenny."

"I love watching him run. Honey, it's just that we have two excellent centerfielders on the same team. Either one would play all the time almost anywhere else."

"Dad, *I* know what!" she said, suddenly brightening. "Let's trade Darryl to the Dodgers for Fernando! We could use a great left-hander, right? Hey, that's funny: a great left-hander right."

"That's the switch-pitcher you've been wanting," I said.

She laughed but quickly stopped herself. "No, this is serious. If we trade Darryl to the Dodgers, then Mookie and Lenny will be able to play at the same time. I feel so sad when one of them has to sit on the bench."

"And I'd feel so sad seeing Darryl hit home runs for fans who leave in the seventh inning."

I thought of my father, who would have had to leave Dodger Stadium in the sixth inning to beat the crowd.

"Maybe you're right," said Lori. "We'd probably miss all the home runs Darryl hits for us. I'll have to figure out something else."

"I'm sure you will," I told her as we walked away from field hockey to continue our meeting of the Hot Stove League.

6
We Don't Care If We Never Get Back

The Grass Is Always Greener at Shea

*E*arly in May 1986, about two months before Lori turned ten, I got a call from my friend Alan Wagner, who is no kin of the composer but a fan of his and an even more passionate fan of the Mets. In fact, Alan is an example of what the supposedly boy's game of baseball can do to an intelligent adult. One Saturday the previous September, he had taken a tiny radio to the Metropolitan Opera to see how the Mets were doing in a crucial game against the Cubs. Of course, a radio at the opera, although less common than a libretto, did make sense. Alan was not sure about the climax of the game, but he knew how *Tannhäuser* came out.

"Would you and Lori like to come to Shea Stadium on Sunday?" he said. "It's the Mets and the Reds."

"Well, we *had* planned to clean up her room," I told him, "but I think we can do that next year. We'd *love* to come."

"Wonderful. Has Lori ever seen a real game?"

"You mean one where they don't throw the ball at each other? No. And her father's last real one was the year the Mets came to the Polo Grounds."

"Then it's time. We'll go early and see batting practice."

"I used to *love* batting practice," I said, remembering that some writer once wrote: "All baseball fans can be divided into those who come to batting practice and the others. Only those who come have a chance to amount to anything." "Is the crack of the bat still a lovely sound?"

"Still music," said Alan.

I had not heard this music for too many years, a shameful absence from the parks caused by the death of the New York Giants, five years later the death of Gramp, and then my move from New York to a state where even the Jersey City Giants had died. On my last trip to the Polo Grounds, to see the Giants play the Mets, I had found tarnished joy in home runs by Willie and Stretch, for I could not accept the Giants as the visiting team in their own park. Moreover, the game had been as big a mismatch as if Camp Wigwam had played Taiwan.

As our Sunday at Shea approached, I could think of little but a major-league ball game where all instant replays would be in my head and the beer would be sold by boys in white hats and not Madison Avenue clowns. And Lori's anticipation grew too. For the last three years, her knowledge of baseball had come from playground games, backyard games, and catches with me that sometimes looked like the start of making fruit salad. But The Game in all its grandness had not yet taken possession of her, and now I wondered again why only baseball had taken possession of me and never football or basketball or quoits. Why was baseball the one boy's game that became a religion for adults? Why could it cause Alan to look at the Rhine but listen to

Kiner? Jacques Barzun had said, "Whoever wants to know the heart and mind of America had better learn baseball." But was the heart and mind of America a bare-chested man singing "The Star-Spangled Banner" and then announcing, "Lasorda, you suck!" Perhaps I would find the answer at Shea.

A few minutes before noon on Sunday, Alan drove Lori and me to the stadium that sat near the site of two World's Fairs. At the '39 Fair, in the Heinz Pavilion, I had been given a small pickle pin and had worn it proudly for many months, as if I had been decorated by a delicatessen; and now, as we walked into Shea, Lori was given a button saying METS and pinned it to her Sarah Lawrence sweatshirt with the same pride that I had felt when wearing my Croix de Caterer.

Built in 1964, Shea was the first stadium in baseball where every seat faced the center of the field and not a single column obstructed anyone's view. My grandfather would have been bothered by the symmetry there, for both foul lines were 338 feet; but my father would have loved Shea's nearness to subways, highways, and two major airports. No park was more tied to escape.

It was, of course, escape of the opposite kind for me this Sunday. With Alan, his wife, Marti, and their two daughters, Lori and I walked up a long ramp, then through a short tunnel, and there it was, a piece of sun-filled splendor that Van Gogh had missed: the American ballpark. And suddenly, I felt the jolt of pleasure, the ineffable nostalgic swoon, that only the first sight of baseball grass can bring to a man of fifty-two. For a moment, I was swept back to the elevated station at 161st Street and River Avenue, where my father had taken me a few times to see the Yankees before Gramp had led me out of the wilderness to the National League. When the train came into that high station, I stood on the seat of the car to catch the first possible sight of Yankee Stadium; and when my father took me back to the station at the end of the seventh, I got up on his shoulders and strained to see any part of the action inside, hoping the train would be late and wondering what the roars were for. I could not see the whole field from that perch, only the infield and only the top half of a home run.

"I wonder who hit that one," I would say.

"You'll read all about it tonight," my father would say to the only boy who went home to learn the score of a game that he had just seen.

And now, four decades later, Lori and I were sitting in a box behind first base, watching the bottoms of flies as well, while batters swung powerfully in the cage and fielders ran and leaped in the grass and I felt a heady return of the boyhood that I had thought ended when Willie had gone.

It was merely batting and fielding practice. It lacked all the dusty action and fierce acrobatics of actual play; it lacked all the suspense of the infinite possibilities too. But my question about the appeal of The Game was already being answered: by the cracks of the bats that cut through the air with the pure sounds of axes in the woods, by the riveting flights of white balls to men who loped to catch them casually and then threw them back with similar grace, and by the scoreboard that had innings instead of a clock, giving me the feeling that time was now suspended for Lori and me. The law of probability said that there *could* be extra innings forever. Lori could marry the bat boy and they could grow old to-gether working on her swing.

When we stood and sang "The Star-Spangled Ban-ner" with fifty thousand people, I felt the tingle that I felt at the end of Frank Capra films; and then the fans began to cheer before the final words of the song and I felt a giddy contentment that Lori and I were here. At this moment, I owed ten thousand dollars to the Inter-nal Revenue Service, termites were salivating over my house, and my dentist had been discussing canals with the glee of Teddy Roosevelt at Panama; but still I knew that today I was safe, that nothing bad can happen to a man at a baseball game, especially when beside him a daughter with mustard-stained lips is demanding, "Let's go, Mets!"

"Our pitcher's name is *Darling*," she said moments later as the Reds came to bat.

"Just like the family in *Peter Pan*," I said.

"This better not be as boring as that."

"Well, we do have a guy who can fly."

And in the bottom of the first, she discovered him as she joined a cry that rose from the crowd:

"*Mooo*-kie! *Mooo*-kie! *Mooo*-kie!"

It was a sound that Margaret Mead might have heard in Samoa, but this tribe was using it to greet Mookie Wilson, with whom Lori instantly fell in love.

"Look how he runs!" she said after Mookie had beaten out a ball to deep short. "Just like *me*!"

"Yes, he's often compared to you," I said.

"He's so cute and fast."

"The two basic things for a player to be."

Unfortunately, the next batter grounded into a double play, which gave Lori new elegance to admire. The second baseman flipped the ball to the shortstop, who leaped over Mookie while whipping a sidearm throw to first.

"That's a double play," I told her. "Two outs at once: you get the man at second and then at first, but you have to move fast."

"It's so *pretty*."

"Just like ballet."

"Daddy, ballet's as boring as *Peter Pan*. This is *exciting*."

"You're right. No one gets knocked down at Lincoln Center."

"Suppose they threw to first and *then* to second?"

"Then there's no force at second and you have to tag him. That's the wrong way to do it."

"But tagging him is more *fun*."

"Not when he's trying to put holes in your leg."

The game was only a few minutes old, but Lori already was loving the beauty of it and the variables that had moved Walter Alston to say, "You just make out your lineup card, sit back, and some very strange things happen."

By the third inning, with her ponytail now tucked under a Mets cap, she knew that a left-handed hitter had trouble against a left-handed pitcher because of the way the curve broke. By the fifth inning, she knew why 3-and-1 was a hitter's pitch, why 0-and-2 was a pitcher's pitch, and why a pitcher when hitting needed Lori's pitch. And by the seventh inning, she knew that a ball bouncing once into the stands was a double and a ball bouncing high in front of the plate was a Baltimore chop.

"A Baltimore *chop*?" she said with a puzzled smile.

"Sounds like something that needs mint jelly, doesn't it?"

"Do they hit more of them in Baltimore?"

"No, I guess they just named it down there—or they didn't. I don't know *everything* about the game, honey. I'm still learning things myself."

"Well, I'm gonna know it all faster than that."

"No, I'm afraid you're not. This is the one game where *nobody* knows it all. That's why Davey Johnson is made of Rolaids."

Not only was Lori being delighted by baseball during this first day at Shea but she was seeing it as if she were helping Alexander Cartwright work out the rules.

"I don't think a bloop hit should count as a single," she said after Dave Parker had dumped one into short right field. "Especially for a guy that big."

"I know what you mean," I said. "It's more an accident than a real hit."

"It should be called a shingle," said Alan, "because it's a hit on the house."

"You see what baseball does to a grown man's mind?" Marti told Lori. "He does better color commentary at *Lohengrin*."

"A shingle would be okay," said Lori, "but he doesn't deserve a whole hit for a little fly that doesn't even reach the outfield."

"But one of these times, he'll have a wicked line drive caught for an out," I said. "There's luck in baseball and it adds to the fun—unless it goes against you. By the way, that kind of hit is called a Texas Leaguer, and you can ask you teacher why."

"The kid already knows more than Howard Cosell," said a man in front of us, turning to Lori with a smile.

"She knew more than Cosell when she was born," I told him. "She's going for Tim McCarver now."

Just then, a bugle sounded a cavalry call and thousands of people cried, "Charge!" The charging, of course, was up to the Reds, who happened to be at bat, but the cry did not have to make sense: it was part of the dedicated nuttiness that intoxicated the fans at Shea.

"Why are they shouting *charge*?" said Lori.

"Just part of the spirit," I replied. "Nice, isn't it?"

"But how are we supposed to charge *now*?"

"Well, we . . ."

"You mean charge the *balls*?"

"I'm really sorry they brought it up."

Once again, the bugle. Once again, "Charge!"

Lori turned to me with a grin.

"Just consider it the motto of the Diner's Club," I said, "until the Mets are up."

The Reds did no charging of their own that half-inning, and now it was time for a richer display of camaraderie. When the Mets came to bat in the last of the seventh, the entire crowd rose and sang the alternate national anthem, "Take Me Out to the Ball Game," a song I had taught to Lori when a fielder's choice for her was a kickball in the kidneys. I felt so sublimely lighthearted singing it now with her and a stadium full of fans that I wished the song would never stop: I wanted to hide in it forever. *This* moment, singing at Shea with Lori while she was falling in love with the Mets and the breeze was rustling her bangs and the sun was shining on a pitchers' battle, was the one to freeze, a moment of such profound happiness that it suddenly made me shiver at the thought of the quick descent to the ten o'clock news.

In the top of the eighth, with the game tied 1–1, Darling walked the first two batters and was relieved by a man who followed a bubble to the mound, Roger Mc-Dowell.

"He's as cute as Mookie," Lori said.

"And his sinker is adorable too," I replied as McDowell warmed up.

"What's a sinker?"

"A curve that breaks sharply down instead of mostly left or right."

"Just *down*? I could hit *that*."

"Yes, with your uppercut, they'd have to throw you a *riser*."

"Can anyone throw that?"

"Just on the moon."

"Then why won't you let me uppercut?"

"Because you're not Babe Ruth."

"Who's she?"

I laughed and gave her a hug. "I'll tell you later; watch Roger now."

McDowell's sinker quickly showed Lori what an art pitching can be: it struck out the next two Reds and made the third one ground to Hernandez. While the fans cheered his work, Lori said, "I love the way he gives that little jump after he pitches."

"The little jump of the ball is much harder to do," I told her.

Anybody *can make a spaldeen drop*, I suddenly heard Morey say. *That's what it* does.

With the insight of Newton, I was struck by the thought that the boys on my block had spent ten years swinging at nothing but *sinkers*. How had *any* of us ever managed to hit a ball above a passing bookie?

In the bottom of the eighth, the Shea bugle began to make more appropriate music.

"Charge!" Lori cried, and then she joined a suggestion that was rising from the stands:

"Let's go, Mets! Let's go, Mets!"

The suggestion was heard by our leadoff man, Darryl Strawberry, who hit the first pitch off the right-field scoreboard for a home run that made me think of Willie McCovey, and also of my grandfather, who would not have said "Another brusher" about Strawberry's ricochet. The scoreboard at Shea was not China, it was Outer Mongolia.

The Mets' one-run lead held up in the ninth, for the man Lori now called her Bubble Baby made each Red batter look like Ralphie batting against Freddie.

After making her momentous discovery of the Mets, Lori began to question me endlessly about them and baseball.

"Did anyone ever drop an easy pop fly?" she said one day during a game of Wiffle ball.

"*Did* they," I said. "The Giants once had a center-fielder named Snodgrass who dropped an easy one that cost them a World Series."

"My Mookie would never do that."

It was her Mookie now, and her Bubble Baby, and her HoJo, with a feeling for them as strong as her feeling for Walden, her gerbil, or Stepper, her guinea pig, or four nameless fish, her goldfish. Lori's heart was full of pets and Mets. Had she known that Whitey Herzog was called the White Rat, she might have been tempted to add him too.

When the Wagners took us back to Shea for a game

against Herzog's Cardinals, Lori eased into her new language. As batting practice began, she turned to me and said, "Gary Carter is really in a clump."

"That's *slump*, honey," I told her.

"A clump is worse than a slump," she said.

What a splendid new word! Not only was my little girl in love with the world's greatest game but she was also coining baseball talk the way Red Barber used to when he spoke of "tearing up the pea patch" and "sitting in the catbird seat." What *son* could have done any better than this third daughter of mine! I felt as elated as if Lori had just won a spelling bee; and she *could* have won a spelling bee, for she knew that there were three o's in Mooo-kie.

A few minutes later, Susan Wagner took Lori down to the field-box railing near the first-base dugout for a closer look at batting practice. Suddenly, one of the Cardinals, an outfielder named Andy Van Slyke, caught sight of Lori's little face beneath her Mets cap, walked over to her, and gave her a ball.

"Here, cutie," he said. "For you."

"Thank you," she managed to say, and then she pressed the ball to her chest, as if she were holding her firstborn, while I silently apologized to the Cardinals for having hoped they would come down with scurvy.

Maybe we can get Van Slyke in a trade, I thought. *It would be nice to have someone on the Mets in love with Lori.*

While Lori caressed her ball, I thought of one that Rabbit Maranville had given to my father when I was twelve, the one he inscribed, "To my pal Ralph." Although Maranville, a shortstop for the Boston Braves, was in the Hall of Fame, I was the only boy in New York who knew it, so my ball drew such remarks as, "Who the hell is Rabbit Manville? A new cartoon?" In fact, six months after I first had brandished the ball to blank young faces, Morey was still saying, "Hey, Ralphie, show us that ball signed by Bugs Bunny." Nevertheless, even though signed by the wrong Hall of Famer, my first major-league baseball was the jewel of my bedroom and caressing it left me as elated as Lori felt now.

When the game began, the Cardinals' leadoff man was Vince Coleman, who had the legs of a cheetah and the mind of one too. Asked by a writer what Jackie Robinson meant to him, Coleman had replied, "I don't know nuthin' 'bout no Jackie Robinson." I had told Lori this story to illustrate both a double negative and also why it was important for a player to know history—if not of the nation, at least of the National League. "If it weren't for Jackie Robinson," I had said, "Coleman's salary might be missing a few zeros today."

"Well, if it isn't Mister I-Don't-Know-Nuthin'-'bout-No-Jackie-Robinson," said Lori as Coleman came up.

"The thing is he runs like Jackie," I said. "He just lacks Jackie's class."

Moments later, Coleman walked and I said, "Now we're in trouble. He leads the league in steals."

"Gary'll throw him out," she said.

"Only if he throws from the mound. And *yes*, Coleman is faster than Mookie."

"Dad, isn't Gary the intensest player we have?"

"Yes, he *concentrates*, which is absolutely the secret of winning. Of course, now he'll concentrate on watching Coleman steal second."

And then the two of us joined Gary in watching Coleman move to second, and he moved to third on a grounder to Teufel.

"HoJo's also intense," said Lori. "Did you see the way he was really ready for that one even though the ball didn't come to him?"

"Yes, I did. I'm glad to see you looking away from the ball. All the fun isn't just in the action."

I was delighted to see her perceptions growing sharper, to see how she was savoring so many of the infinite bits of The Game, to know that I now had a wise companion in this happiest hiding place.

After Sid Fernandez had walked two men to load the bases, Lori said, "Can Coleman tag up on a foul ball too?"

"Fair *or* foul," I said. "Of course, *Coleman* can tag up on an infield fly."

"Except that the batter is automatically out on an infield fly," Susan told her. "With men on base, that is."

"No kidding," said Lori. "I didn't know that."

"Just watch Jack Clark now," I said. "He could be big trouble. He's the one Cardinal who doesn't hit singles."

"We need a triple play."

"Precisely the defense we have in mind."

"Dad, if a guy is thrown out at home and it's the third out, but another guy scores ahead of him, does that run count?"

"Hey, that's a terrific question."

However, before I could answer it, I was distracted by another good one: What had Sid Fernandez thrown to Jack Clark that had just landed in the left-field seats?

"Well, there's your first grand slam home run," I told Lori. "I'm sorry the wrong guy hit it."

"Did anyone ever hit *two* grand slams in one game?" she said, rising above her dismay to continue her education.

"Let's look that up when we get home."

"I could do a report on it for math."

"A pretty short report."

And Lori's pretty short report on that game was: "Bummer."

On our way home, I said to her, "At least you saw some exciting hits today."

"I wish *we'd* gotten some," she replied.

"Next time. But the nice thing is, honey, that baseball is fun even when you lose."

"I'll have to remember that," said Alan as he drove grimly away from Shea.

After dinner that evening, Lori and I went out to the yard for a catch with a tennis ball. Pretending that she was Roger McDowell, she was trying to see if she could pitch and blow bubbles at the same time, the kind of coordination a woman might need to make the major leagues. Suddenly, a bit of bright red swooped across the lawn.

"Look at *that*," I said. "We just can't get away from the Cardinals."

"We've got the wrong birds," said Lori with a smile.

"At least we don't have blue jays."

"Or *orioles*."

"Right! At least we're in the National League."

"Daddy, did any pitcher ever doctor the ball with bubble gum?"

"What would that be . . . a *sticker*?"

"Yes, it would stick to the *bat*."

"And also be kind of hard to get out of the pitcher's hand, don't you think?"

"I better work on it."

During our next game at Shea, one against the Giants,

Lori's feeling for the Mets grew even stronger than mine for the Giants had been. In the third inning, an umpire called Howard Johnson out when he clearly was safe. While Alan and I aired a few thoughts that belonged on subway walls, Lori was silent; and then I turned and saw that her eyes were full of tears.

"Hey, sweetie, don't cry," I said.

"I feel so sorry for HoJo," she replied. "That stupid umpire! Why did he *do* that to HoJo?"

"It probably wasn't personal. Honey, bad calls are part of the game; and if you cry at every one, it'll start to get pretty soggy out here. Look at the bright side of things: you're getting your first look at Dwight Gooden, who's simply the best pitcher in baseball."

"The best *ever*?" she said.

"Well . . . not yet. I still like that title for Sandy Koufax. And not just because he's Jewish."

"Were there any other great Jewish pitchers?"

"He was enough."

Opposing Gooden today was a fine young right-hander, Jim Gott, the kind of pitcher the Giants had needed when Gramp and I used to watch them lose games in which they had hit five or ten home runs. For the first seven innings, both Gooden and Gott had shut-outs; and added to this brilliant pitching was a display of ethereal fielding. Santana threw out one batter while running into left centerfield, Lori's beloved Mookie plucked a ball from the top of the wall, and Hernandez made the kind of play that had moved Charlie Dressen to follow a catch by Willie Mays with the words, "Okay, but I'd like to see him do it again."

"Honey," I told Lori after Hernandez had turned a double down the line into an out, "you happen to be seeing the greatest fielding first baseman in the history of the game."

"*I* know that," she said. "I even told Mommy Keith really fields so *good*."

"So *well*."

"Can't I just learn baseball now and English later?"

"On a day like this, you can."

Lori's spelling, however, was still flawless: every time Gooden struck out a Giant, she raised the right letter, a big red K. And in the last of the eighth, she raised her voice to Howard Johnson as he walked to the plate:

"Come on, HoJo! You're my *baby*!"

"Another baby?" I said. "You're really Mother Met. I thought Mookie and Roger were your babies."

"They have another brother now."

"A pitcher, an infielder, and an outfielder. And two of them switch-hitters; it must be genetic. Maybe you should have a pinch hitter next."

But Lori had no interest in my family planning, she was advising the hitter: "Come on, little HoJo! *Come* on, my baby! Hit one for *me*!"

No prayer in a casino could have been more passionate than Lori's plea to her new baby. And when the count on Johnson went to 3-and-1, she smiled with a dream of a waist-high fastball and said, "Hitter's pitch."

"Hitter's pitch," I replied.

Seconds later, Gott knew it too, for Johnson hit the ball a good way toward Flushing Bay, giving Lori the happiest moment she had known at Shea. While Johnson exchanged high fives with the Mets, Lori exchanged them with the Wagners and me. In fact, she was so exhilarated that she swung her hand one more time after I had dropped mine and smacked me on the nose.

"Oh, Daddy, I'm sorry!" she said.

"That's okay," I said. "We'll have to practice those with your other swing. There'll be plenty more this year. You've fallen for the right team."

And now, in the days and nights that followed this game, Lori's love for the Mets became a rhythm that proved the words of a man named Curt Smith, who said, "Baseball is not a diversion. It is a wondrous dominance." In the evenings, after doing her homework, Lori fought with spunk against sleep by watching as many innings as she could before her big eyes turned smaller. Although the Mets were entertainingly pulling away from the rest of the league, she had to leave the games even earlier than my father used to leave. Sometimes both my arms and the bases were loaded as she groggily said, "Please . . . just this hitter," and I replied, "This one's in the bag, honey. You'll have all the happy details in the morning.

> *"Now run along home*
> *And jump into bed.*
> *Close your eyes*
> *While we're still ahead."*

After tucking her in, I would go back to see baseball's best team continue its superlative play. One night, after Darryl had hit a majestic grand slam in the tenth, I returned to Lori's bed and whispered the news to her sleeping head, hoping it might sweeten her dreams.

On the morning after we had won a night game, I awakened her not with "Good morning" but with "Eight to six, homers for Gary and HoJo, and Roger got the save."

"That's thirteen saves for Bubble Baby," she said through a yawn. "Where's the sports section?"

"Still in the driveway. Look, you have to study your spelling."

"Go ahead, ask me how to spell Dave Dravecky."

If, however, the Mets had lost the night before, I tried to keep the bad news from her as long as I could.

"Morning, honey!" I would say. "What a gorgeous day out there! Say, instead of cereal, how about some nice French toast for a change?"

"How did we lose?" she would say. "I can take it."

"Andre Dawson hit one off Rick."

"Awesome Dawson."

"He's tough to stop."

"We have to get him for the Mets. Him and Jack Clark."

"And let's get Eric Davis and Tony Gwynn in the same deal. Honey, we can't trade for *everyone* who beats us."

No defeat, of course, not even walking in the winning run with the pitcher at bat, could make the sports news worse than the news on the front page. The hole in the ozone was getting bigger and earthquakes were splitting the globe. Things were falling apart both above and below. We had to cling even harder to baseball.

On the day that I read of the widening ozone hole and the chance of the sun growing dangerously strong, I found myself thinking: *Dear God, what kind of sun will be shining on Lori when she tries out for the Mets? Will they have to play nothing but night games then?* Her only practice in playing in the lights has been in our dining room.

At breakfast each day, Lori studied the sports pages of *The New York Times* as if cramming for an exam in baseball, and a sporting stream of consciousness took the place of eating cereal:

"The Cardinals won *too;* we didn't move up. Bummer! ... Timmy is really murdering the ball: three for four. Isn't that *sweet?* I'm so happy for him. ... And my Mookie had a double. Probably a single that he stretched. Dad, you know the two most beautiful sights in baseball?"

"You and your mother at a game?"

"Barfo. They're watching Mookie run and watching a sidearmer pitch. I happen to be a natural sidearmer, you know."

"All baseball knows. Just as it knows that you eat a lousy breakfast."

Turning back to the paper, she read the day's lesson for another few seconds and then said, "Awesome hit *two* against the Reds."

"He hit *three* in one game last month."

"Did anyone ever hit *four* in one game?"

"Yes, a few people. Willie did it, and a guy named Joe Adcock, and a Yankee named Lou Gehrig, and—"

"Oh, *I* know Lou Gehrig. He replaced Wally Pipp."

"Hey, how do you know *that?*"

"I read it when I was supposed to be reading *The Hobbit.* That's such a funny name, Wally Pipp."

"There've been lots of funny names in baseball, like Zeke Bonura and Early Wynn and Bow Wow Arft and Heine Manush. And, of course, Van Lingle Mungo. There's a wonderful song about Mungo that I'll play for you. A guy named Dave Frishberg ..."

But her head was back in her lesson again.

"No *way!*" she suddenly cried.

"What's wrong?" I said.

127

"There's a *mistake* in *The Times*!"

"Please! *Children* are listening."

"Daddy, it says here that HoJo is the seventy-eighth third baseman in Met history. But he's the eighty-*second*."

"When did you learn *that*? During science?"

"It's on the video Susan gave me. . . . But *this* is right: about Roger's sense of humor. It's the greatest one in baseball. He gives the *best* hot foots. Or should that be hot *feet*?"

"I'm not sure," I said. "Proper usage may not apply to setting people on fire."

And so, Lori's first season of loving baseball was one of endless delight, for the Mets quickly built up such a big lead that late in June the White Rat deserted the sinking Cardinals by conceding the pennant to us.

"I don't know nuthin' 'bout no playin' hard the entire season," I said to Lori. "Whitey obviously never heard how the Dodgers were once thirteen games ahead of the Giants in August and still lost the pennant."

"Really?" said Lori. "How did they *do* that?"

"They stank in a hurry."

And then, one Sunday afternoon in July, the gods that governed my life—unless it *was* just one of them—revealed a sense of humor as refined as Roger McDowell's. While I was busy worrying about cosmic catastrophe, they almost destroyed me in a private one.

On that day, Lori, Jill, her husband, Loren, and I were watching a road game between the Mets and the Astros. In the second inning, we all had laughed when a ball bounced over the head of the charging Hatcher for an Astroturf triple.

"They might as well be playing with spaldeens," I said. "Lori, always remember this: baseball is meant to be played in the sunshine on grass, not in a warehouse on cement."

"Mike Schmidt once hit a ball there that bounced off the speaker on the roof," said Loren, "and they held him to a single."

"We used to call that a Hindu," I said. "And a park like this is the heart of Calcutta."

"*I* know what!" said Lori. "Games on Astroturf shouldn't *count*. I think I'll write the commissioner. What's his name, Hubie something?"

"Aren't you also writing to all the Mets?" said Jill.

"Just on their birthdays. I looked them all up."

"That's sweet."

"Yeah, it is, isn't it?"

In the bottom of the fourth, while Ron Darling got into hot water, cooler water began falling from the Princeton sky and I said, "We better put the cars in the garage. The Citation has a sun roof that leaks and the Caprice has a hood that leaks too. It's a special GM design that keeps the engine moist."

Lori was chanting "Bring in Bubble Baby! Bring in Bubble Baby!" as Loren and I went out to move the cars into the double garage. He began driving the Citation into the left side, while I moved the Caprice toward the right; but suddenly, as I reached the center post, I hit the brake, shifted into neutral, opened the door, and leaned out to ask Loren something important, like whether Sisk knew the split-finger fastball. I had forgotten that the Caprice moved in neutral, so it now shot forward, pinning my head between the open door and the center post.

It was a highly creative accident, one overlooked by insurance companies in their lists of domestic disasters; there is no category called "Being Run Down By an Automobile While at the Wheel." A Japanese car would have crushed my skull, but a General Motors car was easily discouraged. This one had creep but no follow-through: it just kept me pinned while I desperately tried to reach the shift to change into reverse, wondering if the end of my life had come. This whole life, of course, did not now pass before my eyes, a screening possible for a mosquito but not a man of fifty-three.

"Help!" I managed to cry.

As a graduate of the University of Pennsylvania, Loren instantly knew when a man was being killed by a car. He dashed like Vince Coleman to the opposite door, jumped into the front seat, and threw the shift into reverse, freeing my head, which obviously had been in neutral.

It was the closest to death I had ever come, a collision with the swirling randomness that left me not just terrified but incredulous at the absurdity of having almost been crushed like a grape while protecting a lemon. It was a moment even worse than when McCovey had lined out to Richardson to end instead of win the World Series of 1962. It was another accident in a world where accidents reigned, a darker version of a ball that took a bad hop.

"Thanks," I told Loren with a certain inadequacy as I took a deep breath to remind myself what living felt like. "I think . . . the moral is . . . never leave a ball game, even when it rains. . . . Look, don't tell the girls about this. If I'd died, you might've had to say something, but . . . well, I don't want Lori to be afraid of parking a car."

When we returned to the house, where Lori now was wearing her Mets hat turned backward as a rally cap, Jill looked at me with concern and said, "Dad, are you feeling okay?"

"Sure," I said too brightly. "I'm always a little nervous when Doug Sisk comes in."

"Doug *Risk*, we call him," said Lori. "I hope Bubble Baby isn't sick."

An hour later, Lori must have wondered why I still seemed happy even after the Mets had lost, and why I was so eager to go outside for Wiffle ball.

Still feeling giddy from being alive, I helped her place Frisbees for bases in a game that would match the 1986 Mets against the 1946 Giants.

"Did I ever tell you about the midget who once came to bat in the American League?" I said.

"Well, what do you *expect* in the American League?" she replied with a grin. "You're kidding, I know, but I bet it *could* happen there."

"No, it really *did*."

"*Really?* A midget in the *major leagues*?"

"Yes, on the old St. Louis Browns. They were almost the major leagues. The owner put a midget in uniform and sent him up to draw a walk, which is clearly a midget's power."

"I'll bet even *Dwight* couldn't pitch to him."

"Right; the guy's strike zone was only a rumor."

"That's what *we* need: some midgets."

"I keep expecting the American League to start using them. Designated dwarfs."

She laughed and then took her position to pitch.

"Okay," she said, "the Giants can hit first, but don't expect much because Bobby O is going for us. Who's up?"

"Bobby *T*."

"Thomson?"

"Right."

"Leading *off*?"

"Right."

"You can't lead *off* with a guy like Thomson."

"You can if you can't remember the guy who really did."

Bobby O held the Giants to just a single in the top of the first; but in the bottom of the first, Sheldon Jones could not hold Lenny Dykstra, who drove a ball so hard into the left-field trees that it stuck there.

"Ground-rule double!" I cried as Lori rounded second.

"No way!" she said, coming in to score. "I never heard of that rule."

"Because you don't follow teams that have trees."

"So that's one-to-nothing. Mookie's up."

"Mookie and Lenny *both* are in?"

"Right, I've benched George Foster for the rest of the year. He stinks."

"He stinks for two million dollars, you know."

"I have to play the best people. I can't be worried about money."

Suddenly, her attention was caught by a stain of red just below the left shoulder of my shirt.

"Daddy, you're *bleeding*. What *happened*?"

With a glance at the blood oozing from the skin I had torn while trying to move a car twenty feet, I said, "Oh, that. It's nothing. Must've been from shaving."

"Your *shoulder*? Daddy."

"Mantle used to play bleeding. The great ones do."

But instead of smiling, she grabbed my hand and led me back into the house and to the medicine chest.

"This is a forfeit, you know," I told her. "Any team that drags the other team off the field ... especially after scoring on a Hindu ..."

"Take off your shirt," she said, and I did, while she opened the hydrogen peroxide. "Daddy, why do you always call a crazy hit a Hindu?"

"It's from stickball: the boys used to call do-overs Hindus. It would sound pretty silly to call them Lebanese—hey, that *stings*."

There was fear in her eyes as she put a bandage on my wound.

"Daddy, *please* take care of yourself. I never want you to ... *you* know."

"Don't worry, honey," I said. "Now that I'm in the lineup, Wally Pipp will *never* get back."

I did not add that my grandfather had made one of his rare trips to Yankee Stadium on a day in 1939 to see Lou Gehrig say good-bye. With a look at the bandage, I knew again that the randomness of life was as scary as the randomness of baseball was wonderful—except, of course, for the shot that McCovey hit at Richardson.

Even with George Foster on the team, the non-Wiffle Mets coasted to the championship of the Eastern Division, and Lori suggested that we celebrate by getting each other gifts tied to baseball. I told her that mine should be a modest surprise and she told me that hers should be a surprise from a list she gave me.

A few days later, with her allowance, Lori bought me a record of Russ Hodges describing Bobby Thomson's home run, while I bought her the first good glove she had ever owned.

"Let's celebrate again when we beat the Astros, and

then again when we win the World Series," she said in early October, trying to set up a sporting version of Hanukkah. "If you lend me ten bucks, I can buy you the video on Willie Mays."

"Buy me a picture of the Polo Grounds instead."

When we sat down the following Wednesday night to watch the first playoff game with the Astros, Lori looked as though her pediatrician had just said she needed a shot.

"We can't lose—*can* we?" she said.

"Only if they get more runs," I replied.

"But we're so much *better* than the Astros."

"I know; it's surprising they don't just concede, but I think we're going to have to play it."

"Daddy, I'm *serious*. We won by nineteen *games*, so this *has* to be a cremation."

"Or a memorial service for us. Honey, if we played them a hundred games, we'd cream them; but in a short series, anything can happen. The Giants swept the Indians in fifty-four after the Indians had won a hundred and *eleven* games."

"Then it shouldn't be a short series. It isn't *fair*."

"You want the World Series played at Christmas? Have the vendors yelling, 'Getcha roasted chestnuts here'? Have Darryl losing fly balls in the snow?"

With a cross between a pout and a smile, she said, "You're right. Only stupid football should be played in the snow."

"I don't want a short series, I want a short *game:* you've got *school* tomorrow. Have you done all your homework?"

"Everything except a drawing of the digestive system."

"Well, let's get that done."

"Do I *really* have to know about the small intestine to be a ballplayer?"

"Ballplayers have to know about guts."

"But not how to *draw* them."

"Come on, honey, just do it. The game'll be late enough; don't skip homework too. Anyway, with Gooden and Scott, you won't have to watch much hitting."

And the game did become so dominated by the pitchers that Lori was able to look away enough to draw the small intestine, pancreas, gall bladder, and liver—not precisely in their proper places, but we pretended that her subject had just taken a shot from Mike Tyson. When she was not reshuffling organs, Lori was rooting from the depths of her own.

"*Mooo*-kie! *Mooo*-kie!" she cried in the ninth, with Darryl on second and Mookie as the Mets' last chance to tie the game. "Do it for *Lori*, baby! Do it for *me*!"

"Come on, Mookie!" I cried. "Do it for the little girl with the kidney-shaped pancreas!"

But Mookie grounded out and then Knight became Scott's fourteenth strikeout and the Astros won. For several seconds, Lori and I sat silently stunned, and then she said, "The split-finger fastball should be illegal."

"Absolutely," I said. "It's immoral too."

"Who do we have who can throw it?"

"Like Scott? No one in the *world* throws it like Scott. I think his ERA is a minus."

"That really stinks. You didn't *tell* me that when I started rooting for the Mets."

"Now *wait* a minute, kiddo. One little loss and you're ready to dump them? Who's your new hero, George

Steinbrenner? My grandfather and I rooted for the Giants for *years* when they were losing."

"Well, I'm definitely not giving them years."

"Will you stay through tomorrow night?"

"Oh, sure."

The following night, her constancy was rewarded: in counterpoint to her English homework, the Mets won.

"Why didn't you do that homework this afternoon?" I said as the game began.

"I had that special meeting for track, don't you remember?"

"That's right; my little jockette, my Queen of the 1996 Olympics."

"I'm not running in the Olympics if it has *boys*."

"Well, I'm afraid there may be a few. What's the problem?"

"Boys are *stupid*."

"Only about half of them. You have some trouble with that half?"

"They keep making fun of girls who can beat them. They do it to me in baseball and they do it in track."

"Honey, they'll grow out of it—a lot of them, that is. You just keep playing the way you do. Men have a problem these days, you see. They used to run the world and they miss it. Just worry about your homework."

"You know, all this homework really interferes with sports. Like why do I have to do so much *English*? I already *speak* it."

In the fourth inning, with no score yet, Lori and I tried to fire up Gary Carter with a version of our favorite Shea chant:

"Ga-*ree*! Ga-*ree*! Ga-*ree*!"

Lori, however, felt that Carter needed more thoughtful inspiration too:

"Gary, if you don't get out of this clump, we're sending you back to Montreal! I don't *care* how cute your curls are!"

When Carter hit the double to drive in the runs that won the game, Lori felt that all was right with the world, even though it was full of English and boys. And two days later, when game three was won by a Lenny Dykstra home run, she vowed to stay with the Mets forever.

"Even if they get a DH," she said after Lenny had circled the bases.

"Then you'll be with them right through next week," I said, "because there'll be a DH in the World Series. And now you see what I meant when I told you that size means nothing in sports. They call Lenny 'Nails' and he's not much bigger than a thumbtack."

In game four, we drew Scott again, and Lori found his splitter so hard to watch that she began a social-studies report that was not due for another week.

"Who could we trade to the Astros for Scott?" she said after he had destroyed us again.

"The infield," I replied.

At once, the two of us started to figure if we would have to face Scott again. I was weak in math, but Lori could count to three, and when she reached it she was dismayed.

"He pitches the seventh game," she said.

"Only if we don't win the next two."

And now the suspense was building the way it had built in August 1951, when Gramp and I had wondered if we could really catch the Dodgers with The Hondo Hurricane on the team.

After Ryan and Gooden had matched strikeouts, game five went into extra innings. In the bottom of the twelfth, the Mets put two men on and Gary Carter came up again.

"I know what he did the other day," said Lori, "but he's still hitting oh-fifty in the playoffs. Is that the worst clump there's ever been?"

"No," I said, "Gil Hodges was in one even worse in a World Series. Something like oh-for-twenty-four. People were praying for him in churches."

"Would a Jewish prayer do any good?"

"It couldn't hurt."

"You know one?"

"Just for starting a meal. I don't know the prayer for meeting the ball. And . . . well, if I said the wrong one, God might be angry and go with the Astros. Their name is already tied to heaven."

"You can't remember the prayer they said for Gil Hodges?"

"We couldn't use it anyway. It was Catholic and you can't switch-hit like that."

While I was wondering if a nondenominational candle might do anything for Gary, our baseball theology was suddenly made pointless by the single he hit to win the game. And this time, I was ready for Lori's second high five and fielded it neatly over my shoulder.

In the history of baseball, there are certain games that have grown into folklore and will be remembered for as long as people come together to try to forget that the world is full of Iranians and lawyers. There was the game that gave us Bobby Thomson's home run. There was the Yankee-Dodger World Series game that became a doubleheader when Mickey Owen dropped a third strike. There was the game between my block and Seventy-sixth Street, in which Morey slipped on dog shit while circling under what should have been the final out.

And there was game six between the Astros and the Mets, the Sistine ceiling of baseball.

Because Lori felt that the Mets now needed her total attention, she unselfishly put them ahead of her academic career and left her homework at school.

"Why tempt myself in a game this important?" she told me.

"You're planning to grow up to be a groundskeeper? Call a friend and get the work. Davey Johnson will understand."

However, once this afternoon game had begun, the two of us were too caught up in it to prepare Lori for college. And by the ninth inning, we were not only caught up but wrung out, for the Mets were down 3–0.

"We have three more outs to avoid facing Mike Scott," said Lori, now as astute a fan as any ten-year-old in America. "You think we can come back?"

"Well . . . you know what Yogi Berra said."

"What?"

" 'Probably not.' "

But suddenly, as we were preparing for a long winter of mourning, Lenny hit a fly that turned Hatcher into a spectator, Mookie singled an inch from Doran's glove, Keith doubled into the gap, Gary and Darryl both walked after countless pitches, and Knight hit the sacrifice fly that incredibly tied the game.

Incredible, however, was about to be redefined. For the next five innings, Bubble Baby allowed only one

Astro to reach first, while Lori kept playing the Shea cavalry call on her clarinet and then crying "Charge!" However, because she was in her first year of clarinet, the call she played sounded too much like "Lazy Mary, Will You Get Up?" to motivate the Mets, so she left the clarinet in the top of the fourteenth and roused the boys with a proper version of the call on her kazoo. Darryl Strawberry, a man who had always seemed attuned to kazoos, quickly responded with a hit and then scored a run that would have been the game had Hatcher not matched it with a shot that hit the foul pole.

"Does that *count*?" cried Lori, bursting with the exquisite agony of it all.

"Just for one run," I told her. "A game of inches, remember? Darryl has hit the pole too."

"Daddy, I can't *stand* it!"

"Yes, isn't baseball a wonderful game?"

In the top of the sixteenth, Lori's kazoo drove the Mets to new heights: three more runs.

"That should do it—right?" said Lori in tentative triumph.

"Well . . ."

"I don't want to *hear* what Yogi said!"

Once again, it was down to three outs, with Lori now too nervous even to play the kazoo, for Bubble Baby had yielded to Jesse and Jesse had yielded two runs. With two out and the tying run on second, Lori grabbed my hand and squeezed it as if I were taking her to her first day of kindergarten. And hand-in-hand, we approached the sixth hour of what has been called the greatest game ever played.

But it was even better than that for a father and

daughter who seconds later saw their Mets win the pennant when Jesse struck out Kevin Bass. Jesse threw his glove in the air and I threw Lori; and when she returned to me, there were no high fives or crazy eights, just one long unhip hug. Greater even than hearing the *Goldberg Variations* was seeing the jubilation of the Mets through Lori's eyes, in the first year when the World Series would be an anticlimax.

Of course, it was not; but it was a Series in which Lori, like a pitcher hanging curves, never lasted beyond the fifth inning because the games were all held in prime time—prime time for beer drinkers, bedtime for kids. And so, Lori saw the first half of each game, and then I walked her to bed while she examined the philosophy of public education.

"It *stinks* to have school in the World Series," she said, climbing into bed in the middle of a scoreless tie with the Red Sox in the opener. "Even *Dodger* fans don't leave this early."

"School is important," I insincerely said.

"Okay, do *you* remember anything you learned in the fifth grade?"

"Well ... actually no. Some African countries, but they all got changed."

"I bet you remember the World Series that year."

"Forty-two? Only that the Cardinals beat the Yanks in five behind Beazley, White, and Lanier, in spite of the Yanks having nine All-Stars."

"And that didn't get changed."

I smiled at the thought of what was in my head in place of knowledge.

"Daddy, don't you love to see an outfielder throw a runner out at the plate?"

"Love it. Great play."

"And don't you love to see a rainbow curve?"

"As much as one in the sky."

"How does a pitcher make the ball do different things just by the way he holds it?"

"I can't really explain it. That's a good one for your science teacher. Now, go to sleep, and only good thoughts tonight. We're in the World Series and we're going to beat the Red Sox."

"And I have to read about it."

What she had to read, however, was how Teufel shuffled a ground ball through his glove to lose the first game.

"He didn't keep his glove on the ground," I told her at our gloomiest breakfast. "*You* could show him how to do that."

"He should *know* it by now," she said, staring at the story in dismay. "And don't tell me to eat."

That evening, she did not have to wait for overnight journalism: She was able to see the Mets fall out of the game by the end of the fifth; and when I tucked her in, she was close to tears.

"We can never win it now," she told me.

"Of *course* we can," I said. "The Red Sox are good at folding; that's what they do *best*. And two years ago, the Royals lost the first two games at home and then came back to take the Series."

I did not add that this event had happened once every eighty-three years.

My frequent feeling that life is a dream might have touched Lori too in the World Series of 1986, for from time to time in the second halves of those games, I left the action, went to her room, and became the only man

in America to share a highlight with someone unconscious. I was hoping that my bedside bulletins about the
good moments for the Mets would somehow be ab-
sorbed by a brain whose last waking thoughts might
have been about defeat or death. And so, when Knight
doubled home two runs in the seventh inning of game
three, I ran to Lori and whispered into her one visible
ear, "Knight, Knight, sweetie. Knight did it."

A few minutes later, after McDowell had retired the
last six Red Sox, I went back to Lori, feeling so happy
for her that I found myself breaking into song, a version
of Loesser's "Rodger Young":

> *"Sound the name,*
> *Every vowel.*
> *Spread the fame*
> *Of Lori's bubbly R. McDowell."*

"You're singing to her while she's sleeping?" said
Judy, pausing at the doorway of the room.

"It's baseball, honey. You just don't know what it
means."

"It means you'll be making the glee club at the Men-
ninger Clinic."

The next morning at breakfast, I wondered if Lori felt
déjà vu from reading about the victory.

"I'll bet you dreamed they had won," I said with a
knowing smile.

"No," she said, "I dreamed about God."

"Tommy Lasorda's coach."

"Daddy, winning is so *great*."

"Definitely better than losing, no matter what Mother
Teresa says."

"Mommy says we make winning too important."

"I know; Mommy thinks they shouldn't keep score. She's a very intelligent woman, but unfortunately not a real American. Don't tell your friends about her."

"I'm hungry," Lori said.

In game four, she went to bed after having seen the Mets take a three-run lead; but I wished she had been with me to see a long drive bounce out of Evans's glove and into the stands. A hardball I had thrown her a few days before had bounced out of her glove the same way and she had said, "That won't happen to me in the majors."

The dream was so real to her, bigger than any dream of God, and again I had let myself wonder if there *was* any chance of my someday hearing the Shea announcer say, "Playing second base, number one, Lori Schoenstein." Her sisters would be there and Loren and also her mother, who would say, "Lori is the *only* one on the team with hair in her eyes."

"And that's why a woman has to be really good to play," I would reply.

On the morning of game six, after the Mets had returned to Shea trailing three games to two, Lori said, "Daddy, can't I *please* watch the whole game tonight? It's *Saturday*."

"Yes, I know, but ... you *do* have to get up early tomorrow to write that big book report *and* study for those two Monday tests. Honey, I always want you to be able to follow all the work at school."

"Lots of kids can't follow it and they don't even like baseball. School comes every day, but the World Series only *now*."

"A good point," I said. "Hey, why am I even *thinking*

144

about something as ordinary as school? Of *course* you can watch the whole game!"

"Yea! Why don't I just stay *home* on Monday? Like you said you did when you were a kid and told them your grandmother died."

"That excuse is gone from baseball, I'm afraid. A kid used to have lots of grandmothers he could kill, but now it's just two and they never die. They play shuffleboard forever in Delray Beach."

In the way that many of us will always remember what we were doing at the moment we heard that John F. Kennedy had been shot, Mets fans will always remember what we were doing at the moment the Red Sox were one strike away from winning the World Series of 1986: we were dying like the grandmothers of yore. I had my throwing arm around Lori, while I searched for the strength to bear the combination of the defeat and her tears.

"But what a *season* it's been!" I said, expecting to hear a band start playing "Nearer My God to Thee."

"Daddy," said Lori, "you told me that the Red Sox always lose."

"Honey, I just don't understand it. Blowing big games has always been such a proud tradition for them."

The poor child was feeling what I had felt when Richardson grabbed McCovey's drive, and what my grandfather had felt when Merkle forgot to touch second and Snodgrass dropped the fly and Lindstrom tried to play a ball off a pebble. Perhaps it was our poignant destiny to be punished this way each October so that we would be tough enough for life's bigger blows. But right now I could not think of one.

At this awful moment in the last of the tenth, with

145

two men out, Carter and Mitchell on base were the tying runs; but dangling hope before Lori when the count on Knight was 0-and-2 would have been cruel, especially with the scoreboard saying:

CONGRATULATIONS RED SOX

Lori and I, however, mad competitors to the end, were hardly ready to congratulate the Red Sox. I, in fact, was still not ready to congratulate the Yankees for 1962. Someone—it was either Leo Durocher or Genghis Khan—said, "Show me a good loser and I'll show you a loser." Although this motto might not have been the best way for me to build Lori's character, I did feel that a fan who graciously concedes to a team that always self-destructs has become too mellow in defeat.

"Well!" said Judy brightly at the doorway. "Are you two having fun with your game?"

Because my arm was encircling Lori, I was unable to get off a throw of the candy dish beside me; but I made a mental note of Judy's words for the judge in our divorce.

Suddenly, as Lori and I tried to believe what we were seeing, a hit and a wild pitch tied the score, the winning run was on second, and at bat was Lori's first love on the Mets, whose number she planned to wear, Mookie Wilson.

Softly, still disbelieving, almost afraid to anger the gods with such a wild request, the two of us began the chant that had begun the season for her:

"Mooo-kie ... Mooo-kie ... Mooo-kie."

After lining a ball just foul past third, Mookie swung

and hit one softly toward first. All right, I thought, at least we've tied it and now we'll win it next inning, or in the sixteenth again, or the game will go on forever, the way that baseball does in your mind.

And then the ball had gone behind Buckner, and ahead for Lori and me was a winter of perpetual spring.

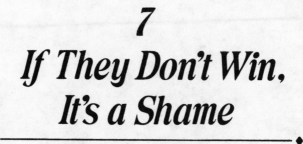

7
If They Don't Win, It's a Shame

But Still Better Than a Stanley Cup

"*T*he center cannot hold," said Yeats, but who cared about football? The glow of being world champions warmed Lori and me throughout that long dreary time of football, basketball, and mugging on ice. When the first snow fell, we were still talking baseball, still savoring the Series, still feeling that the loveliest words in the English language were Billy Buckner. Lori wrote more birthday letters to the Mets, we bounced more balls off the furniture, and we played more games of electronic baseball, sometimes at meals that did not fully hold our attention.

"If you two don't stop that," Judy said one night at the dinner table, "I'm going to start serving only hot dogs."

"Great!" said Lori. "And Daddy can toss you the money."

In early December, Lori made a big drawing on poster board called "All About Roger McDowell," which I renamed "Great Arm with Small Arms." In the drawing, McDowell was holding a firecracker, while tied to his foot was something that looked like a hand grenade. Lori's labels for these two items said: "A firecracker to throw at someone if they say he is scuffing the ball" and

"A hotfoot made by him and HoJo to amuse his team-mates during a loss."

For Hanukkah, she gave me an equally elegant work of art: a *Sporting News* drawing of the Polo Grounds, with notes on its greatest moments.

"That's where Willie made the catch," I told her, pointing to the hallowed spot in Siberia. "You know, Willie loved the game so much that he said he would've played it even if he hadn't been paid."

"*I* love it that much," said Lori. "All I really need is my allowance."

Lori now felt that America was divided into two groups: those who loved baseball and jerks. She was shocked to hear from her sister, who had gone to study art in Oakland, that when Eve-Lynn had mentioned Keith Hernandez at a party one night, the people there did not know if she was talking about a drummer or the president of Mexico.

Incredulously, Lori wrote:

Dear Eve-Lynn:

I didn't send you to California to hang around with people who don't know who Keith Hernandez is. And I can't believe you think the A's are a national league team! I thought you were studying out there!

And then, in what should have been Lori's happiest time, the return of baseball in the spring, she suddenly saw her gods fall off Olympus and into clinics. First, the Doctor turned himself in to other doctors because being the greatest pitcher since Koufax had not been enough of a high for him; but an even more painful blow for Lori was Roger McDowell's hernia repair.

"I'm going to send him a card," said Lori. "And I have to add a hernia to his picture. What is it?"

"A tear in your groin."

"Can you get it from a firecracker?"

"No, it's just bad luck."

And more was ahead. Just a few days later, at the beginning of May, Bob Ojeda went to surgery for his elbow; and before May was gone, so was Rick Aguilera. Incredibly, the day after Rick joined all his pals on the disabled list, his replacement, David Cone, fractured a finger while bunting.

"I can't stand it!" said Lori. "All our pitchers are *breaking*. It's so *unfair*."

Not wanting to remind her of the bitterest truth a child must learn, that life is rarely fair, I tossed her a manager's cliché instead: "Injuries are part of the game."

I knew, however, that *these* injuries were part of a darker game. My friend Norman Corwin, a proud and piteous Red Sox fan whose nightmares included Enos Slaughter, Bucky Dent, and green monsters, had finally snapped at the end of the Series and put a curse on the Mets, and it was working because Norman was part Hungarian. Nonetheless, I was part Hungarian too and should have been able to lift the curse, or at least soften it so that our pitchers merely got sinus attacks. But I could not; and so, when Terry Leach went down a few days later, I had Lori call Norman.

"*Please* take the curse off the Mets," she told him. "I'm sorry about Bill Buckner, but Mookie would've beaten him to the bag anyway. And in the last game, we didn't do anything bad. We just outhit you."

"Well, I'll try, Lori," said Norman, "but a Massachusetts curse is hard to lift. The Red Sox themselves are a curse for us."

By early June, it was clear that Norman had lost the number of his witch; and now Lori's rooting grew even more passionate as she watched her battered Mets try to catch the healthy, crummy Cardinals. During televised games, she began wearing a Mets rally cap with her Van Slyke baseball balanced back of the upturned peak; and once, when Mookie doubled, the ball dropped into a bowl of Rice Krispies and splattered the rug with milk.

"Couldn't she start dropping her baseballs into bowls of fruit?" said Judy that evening. "You know how long the smell of sour milk stays in a rug? For geological periods."

"The problem is the Mets' season may be turning sour too," I said. "And she loves The Game so much."

"Can't she still love it if the Mets don't win?"

"That's what she may have to learn this year."

As the Mets staggered into July, still looking up at Vince Coleman's team, Lori's exhortations turned tender.

"Get me a *run*, you darlings!" she cried one night. "Do it for *Lori!*"

"Or do it for your jobs, you darlings," I said.

"Daddy, I want you to know they're breaking my heart."

"I understand, honey, but we have to remember it's only baseball." She gave me a look of disbelief. "Sorry, I didn't mean that."

"Don't you hate to see Gary have to run? He should be on the DL too. Is there ever a pinch runner who starts at home?"

"There should be one for Gary. It's cruel to make him move his legs."

In her desperate desire to drive the Mets from third place to first, Lori also found time to manage them.

"Why didn't he use *Mazzilli?*" she cried after Magadan had struck out with the bases loaded to end a game against the Cubs. "Doesn't Davey read the *sports* section? Doesn't he know what Mazzilli's *hitting?*"

And the following day, after studying *The Times*, she looked up at me and said, "Can you *imagine* that Davey has HoJo batting *seventh*—after *Gary*—when he has thirty home runs and Gary's been in a clump all year! Dad, can a manager be traded?"

Lori was right, of course, about the value of HoJo's hitting, but there were days when he could have used a designated fielder. In one memorable game, the Mets were leading 1–0 in the eighth and the Astros had the bases loaded with none out. The next batter then hit a one-hopper to HoJo, who decided not to make the trite home-to-first double play. Instead, he went around-the-horn for a triple play that last had been made the year McKinley was shot.

"He almost made it!" cried Lori.

"A stupid play," I said. "He needed Gary running to first. No, he needed The Schnozz."

"Daddy, it's not nice to be mean to HoJo."

"Honey, you play baseball with your head too. This year the boys just aren't doing what I keep telling you is the most important thing: They're not *concentrating*. HoJo has to cut off the run when he's only one run ahead. It'll cost us the game."

And it did. However, in spite of their aching bodies and their porous minds, the Mets kept winning enough to be near the Cardinals when Lori and I returned to Shea with the Wagners for a late-summer game against the

Pirates. On the way to the park, Lori was optimistic.

"The Pirates stink," she said merrily.

I could not bring myself to tell her that we did too, even with our good hitting; but she must have detected an aroma when Barry Lyons went into a reverie and was picked off second to kill a rally that might have won the game. The Mets were having an extended celebration of the World Series.

A few minutes later, Alan took us down to the door of the clubhouse to meet an umpire he knew; and while we were there, Jim Gott, now with the Pirates, walked by. At once, Lori stopped him, looked up a few feet, and said, "I remember you from the Giants. You pitched a good game."

"Thanks," he replied.

"I'm glad you won, but I'm really not—if you know what I mean."

Looking down at Lori's Mets hat, Mets T-shirt, and Mookie Wilson button, Gott smiled and said, "I guess you're not a Pirate fan."

"No, I love the Mets. And we're going to start concentrating more."

Still smiling, Gott said, "If we had your hitters, we wouldn't have to concentrate either."

Although Gott had beaten the Mets, Lori had found herself taking pleasure in the beauty of his pitching and had added him to her list of players to acquire, a list that now held a good part of the National League's All-Star team.

"We've got to build a dynamo," she told me.

"Or at least a dynasty," I said. "But we've already got one. The talent we have just has to increase its attention span to include the game."

In mid-September, when we went back to Shea with Jill and Loren for a game with the Padres, the Mets looked like champions again. HoJo, Darryl, and Kevin hit home runs, no one missed a cutoff man, no one missed a sign, and no one forgot he was running the bases. The only small flaw was Mookie almost falling while drifting back for a fly.

"Remember when Mookie and Darryl ran into each other?" said Lori, as if such a moment were safely tucked in the past.

On that happy day, as she ate rally cookies she had baked, Lori was a bubbly almanac of baseball, sending data in all directions.

"Darryl has thirty-two steals, but HoJo beat him into the thirty-thirty club," she told a young man in rimless glasses beside us, who was wiping mustard from a small girl wearing a picture of Mickey Mouse.

"I wanna see firecrackers," said the small girl, confusing Shea's scoreboard with one in Chicago.

"Oh, Roger McDowell can give you those," said Lori in her teacher's voice; and then she told the man, "He has twenty-four saves already. He just can't stop saving."

"She really knows the game," he told me.

"Yes," I said proudly, "you can ask her anything—except schoolwork, of course."

"Okay . . . who made the only unassisted triple play in a World Series?"

"Bill Wambsganss of Cleveland," said Lori. "HoJo *tried* one with other people this year."

"Very good, young lady. Okay . . . how long was Hernandez's hitting streak?"

"That easy. Same as his number: seventeen."

"A *girl* knows all this?"

"Of *course.* A girl can even know how to strike out Babe *Ruth.* Ask me about the one who did."

"That's enough, honey," I said.

"Daddy," said the man's daughter, "let's go downstairs at the commercial."

Their bond still needed a bit more maturing before it paid the dividends of mine.

By late September, Lori was swinging between elation and despair as the Mets mixed slugging with daydreaming and stayed teasingly close to first. They seemed to have been two games out for the last six months.

"At Thanksgiving, they'll be two games out," I told Lori when the Mets agonizingly lost a game in the ninth the day after they had won one in the same inning.

On September 27, however, they won a doubleheader and a New York headline said:

YO-YO METS GET
BACK IN THE RACE

Suddenly, I was back in the Polo Grounds, seeing the Giants use the ninth inning in the same mind-snapping way. And now Lori's heart had become the yo-yo that mine had been forty years ago, for these Mets *were* the reincarnation of the team that had hit 221 home runs and still managed to lose. Perhaps such coronary capers were even more fun than running away with the pennant, as the Mets had done last year. Surely this was the drama that only baseball, with Orosco failing in relief, could provide.

The drama I did not like this year was the way that some of the world's shabbiness had seeped into The Game with charges about scuffing pitches, corking bats, and throwing beanballs. I feared that Lori might grow disenchanted with what was still the sweetest sanctuary I knew, still the best escape from the world of AIDS and falling planes and the Scarsdale child who had just been run over by her own school bus. I was not, of course, so naïve as to think that The Game had never known man's corruption—there had been the Black Sox, Ty Cobb, and Walter O'Malley; there had been some alternate names for Jackie Robinson—but nevertheless I was dismayed when Joe Niekro was suspended for ten days because an emery board had fallen out of his pants.

"That's the last thing I have to teach you about baseball," I told Lori at breakfast. "Never do your nails on the field."

"I've learned so *much* already," she said. "Remember last night when Ralph Kiner said, 'Teufel has the game-winning RBI so far'? Well, that's exactly what *I* was thinking. So many *times* I get thoughts and then Kiner or Tim read my *mind*."

"Would you rather be a sportscaster than a second baseman?"

"Oh, no, anybody can be a sportscaster. But the first girl at second on the Mets, that's only *me*."

On the final day of this 1987 season, the all-male Mets were still poised to make their move. At Camp Wigwam, at the Polo Grounds, and on the streets of New York, I had known that, even if you lost, The Game was still a wondrous thing. And now, in spite of the activity of her lower lip, Lori knew it too.

At bedtime that night, I lay beside her and read to her "Casey at the Bat." When the poem was over, she said, "That's so sad he struck out. Maybe he had the take sign on those first two pitches."

"Not likely for the cleanup man," I said. "The pitcher had just given up a single and a double to two weak hitters, so Casey was a good bet to cream one."

"But maybe he wasn't cleanup and the manager had him batting seventh like HoJo. The cleanup man doesn't follow two weak hitters, except in the American League."

"A good point, but the take still wasn't likely. Casey just got too cocky. I'll bet he had trouble in free agency that winter."

"What's free agency?"

"A player's right to get overpaid by anyone who wants to overpay him. But there were no free agents in Casey's time ... and no dopey domes ... or green cement ..." And then, instead of forming more words, my tongue began making clicks against the roof of my mouth. "Know what *that* is?"

"Your tongue making noise?"

"Of course not. It's my favorite sound: the crack of the bat. When I was a boy, before TV and the wheel, the sportscasters sometimes did road games from telegraph wire in the studio, so they had to re-create the cracks of the bat and the roars of the crowd."

"They did it with their tongues?"

"No, their tongues weren't as talented as mine, so they had to use a clicker for the bat and a canned roar for the crowd. I used to lie there at night next to my Philco and hear them fake games in Chicago, St. Louis, and Cincinnati. It was strange. It was crude. It was wonderful. ... You know, a guy at Hillerich and Bradsby—they make the Louisville Sluggers—says the aluminum bats are fine because the crack of the bat doesn't mean that much to a kid anymore. You think that's true?"

When she gave no answer, I turned and saw that her

eyes had closed, no doubt from my spellbinding memory of radio. Slipping off her bed, I pulled up her covers and then started out of the room; but passing her desk, I was stopped by her latest letter to a Met:

Dear Mr. Hernandez:

First off I'd like to wish you a happy birthday. I think (I know!) that you are the best first baseman ever. You probably know that too. You're even greater than Lou Gehrig. Of course I never saw him play.

But the real reason I wrote was because I know you might not want to listen, and it's none of my business but I'd like you to please stop smoking. You have great potential and could make it to the Hall of Fame, but I know people who have died from smoking like my grandpa and I really don't want that to happen to you. I wouldn't be writing if I didn't care. Oh! I'm an avid Met's fan!!

By the way my grandpa was a batboy with the Lincoln Giants. They weren't in the national league or the american league either. I don't know which one.

Well, bye now!

Love,
Lori Schoenstein

P.S. I doubt you remember but you signed a picture of me for my sister once last year when you were signing your book!

161

When I left Lori's room, the radio in my head was still playing, now tuned to the World Series of 1945. I was sitting in a music class at Stuyvesant High School and my teacher was walking away from Vivaldi to bring us the prettier sounds of the national anthem from Wrigley Field. The Tigers and Cubs were about to begin something more important than the Baroque. Who could care about *The Four Seasons* when the only season was about to end? Who could care about the Elector of Brandenburg when Prince Hal Newhouser was about to pitch to Swish Nicholson? Swish had been my model at bat: I had always tried to look impressive striking out.

"What a great guy to let us hear the game," I said softly to Morey.

"You got any Trojans?" he replied. "I need a couple."

"You *need* 'em? For Crissake, Morey, this school is all *boys*. Who you gonna nail? The *nurse*?"

"I tell ya, I need a couple."

"We don't *know* any girls—remember? A coupla Trojans'll last you till *college*."

Morey tried to sustain his contraceptive quest, but on that October afternoon no celebration of puberty could have distracted me from The Game. It was lovely to be twelve in 1945, when the American League was still playing baseball and the only dome was Grant's Tomb and hearing a game in a classroom did not mean you were in night school.

But the sounds of that Series now started to fade as I walked through my house more than forty years later, trying to hide from the passage of time, trying not to think about Lori leaving childhood, trying not to hear the last line of "There Used to Be a Ball Park":

And the summer went so quickly this year.

At this moment, as if sensing my mood, Jill called with a message that lifted my spirit: summer was to continue: she and Loren had decided to go to the Dominican Republic, not to do anything as pointless as swim but to make a pilgrimage to San Pedro de Macorís, the town that produced most of the shortstops in professional baseball. How heady it was for me to hear that my daughter was trying to solve a mystery greater than where the elephants go to die or why Atlanta is in the Western Division. On evenings when Judy had tried to turn the dinner talk to such trivia as mental health and international terror, Jill and I had wrestled with this cosmic question: Why do most of the shortstops come from this one Dominican town instead of from Arizona State? And why is Juárez not a natural source of third basemen or Managua a source of right fielders? Darwin had never bothered to ask.

"Jill and Loren are going to the Dominican to look for shortstops," I told Judy that night.

"They're starting a collection?" she replied. "You know, you've all gone insane about baseball. Jill goes into the bush after shortstops and Eve-Lynn buys a car from a man because he played for the Giants and Lori doesn't want to be a veterinarian anymore: she wants to be a ballplayer."

"Isn't that wonderful?"

"*Is* it? Veterinarians don't have to retire when they lose a step going to the cows."

"And ballplayers don't have to sit up with sick sheep. Honey, she's got such a great dream: to be the first woman in baseball, to play second base for the Mets."

"Is she really that good?"

"Well, I haven't seen the scouting reports on other sixth-grade girls, but I know she's the best. She's a contact hitter, she has a strong arm, she's incredibly fast, and she's fiercely competitive. She'd knock down your mother for an extra base and she'd run through a wall for a fly."

"Where did I go wrong? She's supposed to be reading *Little Women*."

"To Lori, little women should be leading off."

A few hours later, while Judy slept, I lay awake trying to hold on to baseball, for the long season of what Lori called dopey sports had begun, the season when giants in shorts would be stuffing balls into baskets and thugs on skates would be stuffing fists into each other. Even baseball at its worst—a high fly lost in the lights of the Astrodome that finally bounced like a spaldeen over Mookie's bewildered head—was better than these dreary games of slam and slash.

For lovers of The Game, the off-season is a kind of death, a word that Lori had touched upon whenever asking me why I had to be older than all the fathers of her friends. I was growing angry at my mother for having launched me in 1933 instead of a more sensible year, like 1948 or 1962. Roosevelt and Hitler had arrived in 1933; the world had not needed me too. And now Lori had put me in a race for my lfe with men who were ten years younger, though considerably more mature. Baseball was timeless, but I contained a clock. How much longer could Lori's happy cries conceal the ticking? How much longer could I keep trying to beat her to the bag? How much longer would there be diamonds for Lori and me?

If I could just have one more chance to hit the ball into Broadway. *Come* on, Freddie, *pitch*.

8
And Suddenly It's Spring

Beyond the Medals, The Game

"*N*ow remember," I told her, "*don't look back*," words I kept hearing from Satchel Paige whenever I wondered where everything had gone. "You're running a *race*, not an escort service."

It was spring again, just a week before Opening Day, and we were at the Princeton Junior Olympics, where last year Lori had won a silver medal instead of a gold after losing a fraction of a second to a survey that she had taken of the other runners in the fifty-yard dash. The Princeton Junior Olympics was one of the two major track-and-field events to be held this year. There would also be one in Korea, but to Lori, Korea was the part of the Polo Grounds with the scoreboard, just above the seats of Japan, that she had learned of as the first child to hear bedtime stories about Willie Mays.

It was spring again, and the rebirth of the world distracted me from the vanishing ozone, the melting polar ice, the candidates for president, and my fear that the sun was somehow going to die, possibly in disgust at all it had been forced to shine upon. The death of the sun, of course, would be an advantage for the Mets because all their games would then be played at night, when Gooden, Fernandez, and Myers were hardest to hit.

It was spring again, and Mooo-kie was restless, Rafa-yell was gone, Doug Risk was gone, hum babe no longer belonged only to my past, and Lori was leading the John Witherspoon varsity softball team in both hitting and falling down.

"I'm running against Rhonda again," she said now with a frown as she took off her Mets jacket on the Junior Olympics field. "Rapid Rhonda."

"You'll beat her this year," I said. "You grew over the winter and she looks the same size to me."

"Yeah, enormous. Did you see her in that first heat? Those *legs* . . ."

"It's not the length of your legs that counts."

"Then why did you say I grew more?"

"Well . . . mentally too. You now know to face only in one direction."

"Rhonda's *always* known that."

"What a clubhouse *lawyer* the Mets are going to get! You'll be the first rookie free agent. Anyhow, you would've beaten her *last* year if you hadn't socialized."

"Mom told me just enjoy the race."

"*You* know Mom puts too much emphasis on peace."

"Well, I'm gonna *destroy* Rhonda today."

"Atta girl. But be a good sport. And don't tell Mom I said this, but have fun."

"I'll run like Vince Coleman if he was nice."

I looked at her T-shirt and smiled. "You know, I think we made a mistake with that shirt. Everyone else is wearing . . . well . . ."

"But I *represent* the Mets."

"That you do."

And then the announcement sounded across the field: "Eleven- and twelve-year-old heat winners to the track for the final of the girls' fifty-yard dash."

I gave Lori a kiss that she probably hoped no one saw and then I retreated to the stands as she walked to the starting line, my last daughter in her last year of innocence, for her hormones were running too.

While Lori and the four other finalists assembled for the race, I remembered my own last display of the spirit that was driving her now toward this finish line and toward the Mets: at a tennis club last week, I had played a lawyer of sixty-seven, a former singles champion. Because I was thirteen years younger, I had wondered as the match began: Should I try to beat him by running him or should I patronizingly play a mediocre game, which came easily to me?

After deciding that Leo the Lip would have wanted me to do my best, I won the first two games with placements that I rationalized as aids to the lawyer's circulation. In the third game, however, he beat me, making me happy for him. When he beat me again in game four, I was less happy for him; and when I lost game five, I thought, *Okay, you ambulance chaser, get ready for an ambulance to chase you!*

The match was now a clash between the arms of a former champion and the legs of a man who ran against his daughter. It was five games for his arms and five for my legs when he suddenly stopped and put a hand to his head. At once, I ran to his side of the court, going around rather than jumping over the net because the score was still tied.

"I think . . . I'd better quit here," he said between quick breaths.

171

"Of course," I said, graciously not mentioning that he had defaulted. "I'm sorry about all the running; I'm so used to racing my little girl. I never seem to be with my own age."

Sitting now at the Junior Olympics and still dreaming of one more try to hurdle the iron bars of Broadway, I wondered if I was headed for the sideshow of some circus to be displayed as The World's Oldest Child.

Crack!

The sound of the starter's gun shattered my reverie and I quickly focused on Lori. This year, she made no checks on progress in the other lanes, but instead flew down the track with the legs I had misplaced and finished one stride ahead of Rhonda to win her first Olympic gold medal.

Within seconds, I was at her side, easily beating two other fathers in the congratulations dash.

"You *did* it, darling!" I cried. "And you never looked back!"

"I knew Rhonda was close," she said. "I wanted to slide."

It was then I knew that, from this day on, whether tempted to slide into finish lines or uppercut pucks or shoot split-finger layups, Lori would never stop thinking about The Game.

After an early, half-eaten dinner, we were in the backyard again. Judy had wanted Lori to call her two grandmothers about the gold medal, but Lori was hearing the call of The Game.

"Don't think that we '47 Giants are impressed by your speed," I said as she brought the '88 Mets to bat. "Jackie Robinson didn't scare us and neither do you."

"I'll bet he stole you blind," she said as she took her stance with her Super-Pro blue plastic bat and I picked up a Wiffle ball. "Who's pitching?"

"Clint Hartung," I replied.

"*Hondo* Hartung? He was a *pitcher*?"

"He played a *lot* of positions badly."

"So why aren't you using Oslo or Jansen?"

"*Koslo*, and we're saving him and Jansen for our series with the Braves."

"We'll *cream* Hondo!"

"*Cream*?" I said. "We're the *dairy*. We're on our way to hitting two hundred and twenty-one home runs. We've got Big Jawn Mize, left-handed power who makes Darryl look like a Dominican shortstop."

"*No* left-hander can hit Randy Myers."

"Are you *kidding*? You think Mize made the Hall of Fame in a *platoon*?"

"Okay, play ball!"

"Who's leading off?"

"Raf—I mean Kevin," said Lori with a frown. "I *hate* all the stupid trades. You think any more stars will be going to Japan?"

"Well, I don't know about *your* team. Mine goes to Mexico."

"No, *really*. The paper says some stars may be playing for a lot of money in Japan."

"Then there'd be room faster for *you*."

Her frown reversed into a smile. "Yeah, I never *thought* of it that way!"

"Okay, batter up; Hondo's ready."

I looked hard at the batter, this aggressive beauty, this beloved jock, poised to pounce on the pitch at home Frisbee, and then I delivered. Seconds later, I remembered why Hondo had never quite worked out, for Lori swung and hit one of the longest drives of her short career: a ball that landed in the green monster in left centerfield, a group of tall oak trees. A *group*, not a clump. When we are out at the old ball game, Lori and I can never be in a clump.